Economics
and Ethics

ECONOMICS AND ETHICS

An Introduction to Theory, Institutions, and Policy

DOUGLAS VICKERS

PRAEGER

Westport, Connecticut
London

Library of Congress Cataloging-in-Publication Data

Vickers, Douglas, 1924–
    Economics and ethics : an introduction to theory, institutions,
and policy / Douglas Vickers.
        p.   cm.
    Includes bibliographical references and index.
    ISBN 0-275-95978-3 (alk. paper). — ISBN 0-275-95979-1 (pbk. :
alk. paper)
        1. Economics—Moral and ethical aspects. I. Title.
    HB72.V498 1997
    174'.9339—dc21   97-5594

British Library Cataloguing in Publication Data is available.

Library of Congress Catalog Card Number: 97-5594
ISBN: 0-275-95978-3
        0-275-95979-1 (pbk.)

First published in 1997

Praeger Publishers, 88 Post Road West, Westport, CT 06881
An imprint of Greenwood Publishing Group, Inc.

Printed in the United States of America

The paper used in this book complies with the
Permanent Paper Standard issued by the National
Information Standards Organization (Z39.48-1984).

10 9 8 7 6 5 4 3 2 1

CONTENTS

PREFACE

One of the more important developments in economics in recent times has been the breaking down, as Vivian Walsh has referred to it, of the "barriers to fruitful exchange between economic theory and moral philosophy" (1987, 3:868). The possible two-way conversation is not yet at full flood. But recognizing those newer lines of development, I have aimed in this book to bring into clearer focus the necessity for, and the possible range and effectiveness of, an expanded conversation between economists and moral philosophers.

Economic theory, as it matured from its classical foundations through the neoclassicism of the later nineteenth and early twentieth centuries, surrendered its earlier moorings in the ethical and philosophic foundations from which it had developed. The methodological revolution that Ricardo accomplished at one end of the nineteenth century effectively extruded the ethical from the ethico-economic discourse that had characterized the nascent discipline. And Walras and the neo-Walrasian revival at the other end of that century, making economics substantially a matter of mathematical technique, effectively divorced the subject entirely from its erstwhile ethical presuppositions.

My objective, accordingly, is to raise the possibility of establishing new and more substantial bridges between ethical philosophy and economics. With that end in view, I have structured my argument in a manner that addresses three main issues: first, the historical respects in which economics has consciously surrendered its association with ethical categories and criteria; second, the need to articulate, in a brief and substantially nontechnical manner, the relevant thoughtforms and vocabulary of ethical theory; and third, the illustration of areas in economics where ethical awareness is desirable and should be allowed to exert its influence.

The structure of the book and the order of development of my argument are indicated more fully in chapter 1. Following that introductory chapter, the main body of the work is divided into two parts, the first of which discusses the present status of economic and ethical theory. The three background chapters of that part describe, first, the manner in which, at the hands of the principal architects of the discipline, economic theory witnessed a fairly substantial dissolution of an earlier ethical ideal; second, the vocabulary and relevant concepts that have been developed by moral philosophers under the headings of meta-ethics and normative ethical criteria; and third, the argument as to whether economics is, or can be, or should be, a value-free enquiry.

The four chapters in the final part of the book examine three main issues: first, the relevance of ethical criteria for activity on both the supply and the demand sides of markets, taking account in those contexts of marginal criteria and the highly important contributions to economic theory of philosophic utilitarianism; second, the question of income and wealth distribution and the extent to which considerations of distributive justice can or should impact on economic argument; and third, relevant issues of macroeconomic policy and performance.

In taking account of the recent widening and to some extent the deepening of the conversation between economists and moral philosophers, I have endeavored to give full acknowledgment to scholars who have preceded me. My book, while it aims at the desirable economic feature of product differentiation, might be seen as complementary to a small set of works that similarly aim at refurbishing the ethical foundations of our subject. Sen's brief but challenging *On Ethics and Economics* (1987), Rothschild's *Ethics and Economic Theory: Ideas, Models, Dilemmas* (1993), and Buchanan's *Ethics, Efficiency, and the Market* (1985) have influenced my own approach to the subject. In the chapters that follow, the issues they have addressed are explored, and an extensive literature that deals with relevant aspects of both the philosophy and the economics of our subject is acknowledged.

I am conscious that widely different perspectives from those I have adopted, different issues from those I have explored, and different selections of arguments and critiques that already exist in the literature might have been addressed. It is clear, as the initial chapters will suggest more fully, that economics as an autonomous discipline has developed in a manner that has distanced it from contact with ethical considerations. If I have effectively opened the way in this book to eliminating some barriers to ethico-economic understanding, it will be clear that a much larger work than the present one remains to be written. That larger work will further probe the technical issues of economic analysis that I have deliberately set aside. I have addressed the more modest task of raising questions of ethical desiderata and criteria and opening the way to the perception of areas of economic application. I am conscious that a great deal of what remains to be done is not directly addressed in the present work. But I hope that the framework of analysis that is presented will be useful to economists and other social scientists in coming to grips with the issues I raise and those further explorations that are provoked by them.

This book stands in relation to my previous writing that presents a critique of the development and the present state of economic theory (see References). I have argued that economics has been impoverished by the failure to take account of the phenomenon of real historical time within which economic decisions and actions occur. The real-world context of market behavior has not been accorded adequate explanation, by reason of the concentration on timeless, equilibrium theoretic analysis and on what I have referred to as pseudotemporal dynamics. In several respects also, an identifiable range of ideas and concepts has had a tyrannous hold over economic analysis and has called in question the cogency and the relevance of conventional market theory. Those ideas have to do with the questionable nature of marginal optimization criteria on both the supply and the demand sides of the markets for commodities, productive factors, assets, and money. The present book, moving beyond those levels of analytical critique, argues that economic discussion and the explanation of market activity remain incomplete until relevance is accorded the contributions that emanate from ethical philosophy. The latter throw their light on the practices and outcomes of economic affairs.

I have incurred a heavy debt to several scholars in the construction of this work. While I absolve them from responsibility for the use I have made of their very helpful advice and comment, I record my deep gratitude to Professors James Crotty, Donald Katzner, and Stephen Resnick. My thanks are due also to Ann Hopkins who provided insightful editorial guidance.

Part I
Introduction

1 ECONOMICS IN ETHICAL PERSPECTIVE

Economics in its theoretical and pragmatic expressions has been diminished, I argue in this book, by the surrender of its moorings in moral philosophic foundations. Ethical categories, as the moralists see them, and economic arguments exist frequently in uneasy tension. To observe that that is so is in danger, of course, of stating the trite and the commonplace. For in the progress of both the natural and the social sciences, issues of efficiency and ethics collide. In the former, for example, the technical capacity to develop instruments of mass destruction confronts issues of the morality of their use. On another level, the objectives and the technical potentialities of fetal research collide with issues of the morality of fetal abortion. Examples could be multiplied.

In economic argument, to the extent that it is consistent with received analytical traditions, the consideration of efficiency is generally paramount. Producing firms aim to achieve optimum levels of technical and economic efficiency that provide maximum attainable outputs for given levels of factor inputs, or minimum expenditures on inputs for specified levels of output values. For the consumer, the efficiency objective calls for the achievement, for specified outlays, of a maximum attainable level of satisfaction. The latter is frequently denominated utility, as that is implicit in consumers' preference orderings over objects of choice. Rational behavior proceeds in terms of decision criteria inherent in the formulated objective functions and in satisfaction of what are generally a well-defined set of axioms of choice or action. The firm maximizes a profit or an economic value function subject to resource availability constraints, and the consumer maximizes a utility function subject to an income or wealth constraint. Considerations of economic efficiency in these respects proceed against the assumptions of well-defined and exogenously given objective functions and what may be referred to as autonomously defined decision makers or choosers. Economic behavior and choice decisions in the marketplace are then, against those assumptions and criteria, sanitized from, or their calculation is generally untarnished by, explicit ethical criteria. Economics and ethics have become substantially disjoined.

Our subject is rescued from the commonplace by the seriousness of the ethics-efficiency tensions that exist for both individual behavior and, more generally, societal constructs. My aim in this book is to address a number of issues that arise from these realities. My first concern will be the manner in which economic argument has drifted away from its earlier relation to ethical desiderata, or the respects in which the ethical has been extruded from the ethico-economic discourse that earlier characterized the discipline. Second, a brief address will be made to the manner in which the attempt to maintain a cleavage between normative and positive economics has abetted the aspirations of economics to scientific status, and in doing so, has underlined and confirmed the extrusion of the ethical. Third, a review, in language that is shorn of excessive technicalities, will be made of meta-ethical and normative ethical categories in order to consider their relevance to economic argument. Fourth, categories of argument will be proposed within which economic theoretic and policy questions might be examined. In that manner, it is aimed to illumine the intersection of ethics and economics, and to propose lines and directions of behavior and policy action.

In pursuing these objectives, arguments on a number of differing levels will become inevitably intertwined. It is necessary at points to digress briefly, taking note of some technicalities of economic analysis, as a background to issues of ethical relevance. The objectives and behavior of the business firm are examples of this on one level. Other examples include the examination of the objectives and theory of income and wealth distribution and the cognate theory of economic welfare.

Again, it will be necessary on occasion to suggest new ways of looking at the scope, the objectives, and the procedures of economic analysis itself, in order to bring into focus what might be thought to be more clearly acceptable ethical criteria. It will be necessary to question whether different ways of looking at economic structures and institutions might better address questions of social and civic morality. For these reasons, it will become clear at points in the following chapters that the question of ethical criteria of economic conduct is intermeshed with that of how the economy works, or how, on grounds of certain criteria, it should work or might be made to work. Economic argument and ethics, as they cannot be sanitized and kept strictly apart, will be mutually influential in the following argument.

An important disclaimer is necessary at this initial point. It is not aimed or intended to provide in the following chapters an exhaustive analysis of the interconnection and interdependence of ethics and economics. Nor is it intended at this stage to be exhaustive in either the details of the relevant economic analysis or the applicable ethical philosophy. As Buchanan wisely and modestly observed in his insightful work *Ethics, Efficiency, and the Market* (1985, 1), "such a task could not be completed in one volume, nor by one author." If, as will be argued, a serious reappraisal of economic argument is called for, an important task exists in laying new foundations, or, in more modest terms, in providing some building blocks that might be thought to be appropriate for foundation building.

A BRIEF HISTORICAL PERSPECTIVE

The relations between ethics and economics that existed at the foundation of the latter discipline are inevitably distorted by the mists of historical interpretation. But morality and the marketplace were early joined in a tension that philosopher-economists resolved only reluctantly in favor of continuing economic expansion. The attempt to maintain a social status quo was in due course surrendered, and the medieval manor was soon beyond recall. Economics became more than a laying down of relevant moral axioms. The retreat of trade horizons and the maturing market system, developed and exploited by mercantilist adventurers and financial capitalists, soon changed forever the structure of social and economic relations. And all too soon, it seemed, morality itself, or the moral sensitivities that informed the nascent economics discipline, had also retreated.

It is pointless, of course, to suggest that the structures and systems of thought of that prescientific economics might repay recapture, in the sense that they could again determine economic life situations. The development of the market, with its division of labor and productive specializations, has conferred and confirmed its benefits in human betterment. But the impact of commerce on culture in the centuries between Aquinas and Adam Smith raises questions of ethico-economic relations that warrant renewed investigation.

It is true that at the beginning of systematic economics a sense of moral imperatives informed the subject. Adam Smith had produced his *Theory of Moral Sentiments* some two decades before he published his *Wealth of Nations* that transformed the discipline and gave birth to the English classical system. It is equally true that the notions of benevolence and human sympathy that the earlier Smith had proposed were to a large degree submerged, or lived only an indirectly influential life, in his second great work.

Other classical authors, notably Thomas Chalmers who sided with Malthus in the after-effects of the Godwin-Malthus debate, were acutely conscious of the ethical substratum of economic thought (see Waterman

1991; Hilton 1988). Chalmers, who occupied the Chair of Political Economy at St. Andrews University before assuming the Chair of Theology at Edinburgh, was regarded by John Maynard Keynes as one of his significant anticipators. Keynes's assessment turned principally on the fact that Chalmers joined his friend Malthus in arguing against the automatic applicability to economic analysis of Say's Law. But his claim to fame rests to a good extent also on his extensive writing on the relation of ethics to economics. One commentator, J. Wilson Harper, has suggested that Chalmers was the most important writer on that level since Thomas Aquinas (1910, 7).

But it is beyond doubt that a dissolution of the ethical ideal occurred between, say, Ricardo at the beginning of the nineteenth century and Walras at its end, or the neo-Walrasian developments that have occurred in more recent times. By the end of the nineteenth century the divorce of economics from ethics was fairly complete. That is true, even though a large amount of work by the neoclassical economists in the later nineteenth century exhibited an acute social conscience and addressed important issues of social and economic policy (see Hutchison 1953 and 1964, ch. 1). John Stuart Mill in the middle of the century constructed his *Principles of Political Economy* in a manner that evinced a concern, as the full title of his work indicated, for "their applications to social philosophy" ([1848] 1961). The principal architect of the more fully developed neoclassical system, Alfred Marshall, whose dominating influence continued into the twentieth century, laced the chapters of his *Principles of Economics* with issues of social concern. And others among the neoclassical economists, notably Sidgwick whose claim to fame rests also on his work in the history and theory of ethics (1931; [1874] 1962), kept the ethical import of the subject in view.

Nevertheless, the philosophic influences that formed the intellectual climate of the age abetted the rush to establish a value-free enquiry and to separate from economics the impact of ethics and its normativities. In the later nineteenth century, positivism substantially triumphed. Positivist-scientific economics should not be tarnished, it was increasingly argued, by normative instrusions. That tendency is clear from arguments advanced by some prominent opinion-formers in the subject.

Pigou began his influential *Economics of Welfare* ([1932] 1962) by taking note of the bequest that economics had inherited from the earlier mainstream of utility theorizing. He gave some space to sorting out, as he saw it, the terminological confusions that existed between "utility," "intensity of desire," and "satisfaction." But, as he said, "the verbal issue is a subordinate one." What was really at issue was Pigou's wish to invent a term, such as that of "desiredness," which, he suggested, "cannot be taken to have any ethical implication" (23). In Pigou's conception, a sanitized distinction needed to be preserved between economics and ethical presuppositions and criteria.

John Neville Keynes, the prominent Cambridge economist at the end of the nineteenth century, published what became the standard methodological treatise in economics. In it he confirmed the separation of the normative from the positive in economic argument (1891). Lionel Robbins addressed the same distinction in his classic *Essay on the Nature and Significance of Economic Science* ([1935] 1948), and he expanded his argument to remark explicitly on the relation between ethics and economics that we now have in view. Robbins complained against those economists who "argued that Economics should not only take account of valuations and ethical standards as given data . . . but that also it should pronounce upon the ultimate validity of these valuations and standards." His contemporary, Ralph Hawtrey, had suggested, unwisely in Robbins's view, that "Economics cannot be dissociated from Ethics" ([1935] 1948, 147–48). Robbins's own conclusion, which was itself to remain highly influential in the analytical development that followed, was that economics "is fundamentally distinct from Ethics" (152). Robbins's position was effectively confirmed by the subsequent and widespread mathematization of economic analysis, precipitated notably by Hicks's *Value and Capital* ([1939] 1946) and Samuelson's important *Foundations of Economic Analysis* (1947).

These positions have had continuing and even determinative influence in economic analysis. More recently, Friedman's "The Methodology of Positive Economics" (1953) has taken a comparable stance. It is of considerable interest that the extensive debate, discussion, and critical evaluation that Friedman's work provoked were focused almost completely on his claim that the test of the validity of an economic theory had to do with its predictive competence. The realism of its premises was not of primary concern. Of immediate moment is that Friedman's essay, in making its strong positivist claims, argued that "positive economics is in principle independent of any particular ethical position" (1953, 4). But that claim for the separation of economics from ethics was substantially unnoticed, or was not commented upon as a matter of significant interest, in the ensuing critical and controversial literature.

By the mid-twentieth century, any connection that might previously have existed between economics and ethics had been fairly definitively dissolved. The claim made by Heyne some two decades ago, that "the complacent consensus [that economics and ethics should remain distinct] has been loudly shattered" (1978, 183), has in the event turned out to have been premature. But Heyne did identify a significant direction of movement of opinion. The stream of conversations between economists and moral philosophers has not yet become a flood, but significantly, as Vivian Walsh has recently observed, the "barriers to fruitful exchange between economic theory and moral philosophy . . . are down, and the honest confrontation of the issues which properly concern the moral sciences can relieve economists from the shameful pretense of ethical neutrality" (1987, 3:868). We hear in this the echoes of Adam Smith's friend, the philosopher David Hume, who observed that "we cannot reasonably expect that a piece of woollen cloth will be brought to perfection in a nation . . . where ethics are neglected" (1964, 3:301).

McPherson has observed in a recent essay on "Reuniting Economics and Philosophy" (1988) that there is no longer any need for economists "to regard any hint of moral judgment in their work as a derogation from professional standards" (71). At the same time, of course, strenuous arguments have continued to defend an earlier orthodox position, or the insistence on ethical neutrality and a normative-positive distinction. Those advanced by Klappholz ([1964] 1984, 276–92) and Hutchison (1964) will be noted again in the following discussion.

Part of the reason, no doubt, for the lateness of the new association between economics and ethics has been the uncertainty of the moral sciences as to where they stood and what bequest they might make to other disciplines. As philosophy turned from system building of an earlier style to questions of language and meaning, so the thought forms and vocabulary of ethics attracted intensive scrutiny. For that reason the discussion in chapter 3, heavily compressed though it is, is designed to provide an initial sorting out of relevant foundation concepts and terminology.

SOME RELEVANT ISSUES IN ECONOMIC ARGUMENT

A number of issues will determine the form that the analysis in the following chapters takes. Prominent among the formative influences on economics was the commitment that the subject made to varying forms of utilitarianism. Embraced thereby were forms of teleological or consequentialist ethics. That development, it will follow, raises the need to address related issues of equity and equality, of self-interest and selfishness, and of economic justice and welfare.

The points at which ethics has potential impact on economics will be traced also through the marketplace and through alternatives of macro-market developments. Our interest is in the operation of what early became a monetary economy. Marshall, in his architectonic *Principles*, brought the subject under the measurement of money (1920, 14–22). Pigou, who succeeded Marshall in the Chair of Political Economy at Cambridge, also spoke explicitly of "the measuring-rod of money" ([1932] 1962, 11). In the analysis of market activity money was the medium of exchange that enabled the trading system to cohere and to achieve a high level of productive and distributive efficiency. In the context of the monetary market economy, questions of social ethics will be seen to reside in such areas as the distribution of rewards for work, the rightness or wrongness of property entitlements or property rights, the provision of equality of opportunity, the presence or absence of economic discrimination, the concentrations of economic power and the exploitation of them that clog the system, and the wider distribution of both the economic costs and the economic benefits of what the nation produces.

An evaluation of the functioning of the market system calls not only for a consideration of technical efficiency. It has to do also with the respects in which socially optimum results are or are not realized when they are assessed against suitably defined ethical criteria. The responsibility of work, of productive effort and its social contribution, comes to the fore. But equally, the question needs to be addressed of why conditions arise in which, due to the malfunctioning of the economy, there may be no work for people to do. Morality exists also on the level of aggregative economic policy and objectives.

The question of what the economy produces, quite apart from that of the technical efficiency with which production is accomplished, contains a clear and pressing ethical implication. It touches the issue of the rightness or the reasonableness of the distribution and allocation of the nation's economic resources and the needs they are directed to meet. At issue is not simply the possibility that the economy may be brought, with the assistance, perhaps, of greater or lesser degrees of official intervention, to a situation of the full employment of the nation's resources. At issue also are the questions of what it is to which those resources are allocated and what they are used to produce. Ethical criteria, or what we might envisage as issues of macromorality, inform the choices that are made between guns and butter, or between consumption goods of one kind or another and investment goods and capital formation. They have to do with the establishment and maintenance of economic and social infrastructure, and at that point the intergenerational transfers of benefits and costs also become relevant.

On the level of technical analysis, an ethical dimension inheres in the relation between the ideas of marginal productivity, marginal valuations, and factor rewards. For these ideas point to a theory of income or benefit distribution, on the level of which an ethical intrusion occurs. J.B. Clark, for example, one of the foremost proponents of marginalist principles in the United States at the height of the neoclassical period, has been justly renowned for his suggestions that linkages existed between social proprieties and the rewarding of factors of production in accordance with their marginal productivities (see Clark [1899] 1956). Joan Robinson also has addressed the question of the exploitation of the providers of factors of production, concluding that exploitation occurs when such individuals are rewarded at a rate less than the marginal products of the factors ([1933] 1969).

Issues of ethical import arise on both the demand and the supply sides of the market. The propriety of the structure of firms, the status and interests of the providers of labor services and capital respectively, and their shares in economic profits and losses bear on our subject. Questions of the rightness or wrongness of industrial management conduct; the rewards that management personnel receive, frequently in comparison to other factor rewards in the contemporary context of corporate downsizing; the responsibilities of management to shareholders, creditors, and external social interests; and the justification or otherwise of income distributions, all sustain ethical dimensions. On the demand side of the market the long history and the ethical import of utility and utilitarianism call for examination.

FIVE DICHOTOMIES IN ETHICO-ECONOMIC ARGUMENT

The discussion of these issues in the following chapters will incorporate at appropriate points a review of some historical debates, such as those, for example, that produced the nineteenth-century utilitarian theories and the famous *Wertfreiheit* discussion. But such digressions into the intellectual history of the subject will be intended to serve the establishment of critical perspective and will not be extended for their own sake. They will not, therefore, make any claim to completeness.

The critical and evaluative positions that are taken will be determined by the content and relevance of five dichotomies. These may be adumbrated briefly as follows.

Individuality and Solidarity

Ethical criteria bear forcibly on individual decision and action. The very questions that ethicists have raised: "Where does ethics come from?," "How ought I to live?" (see Midgley and the extensive discussion in Singer [1991] 1993), or what is right behavior or the nature of obligations that should properly be observed, all impinge in one way or another on individual conscience and decision. Self-interest, selfishness, or altruism may exert their influence on behavior outcomes. And the objectives of actions that are taken might embrace greater or lesser degrees of recognition of social and cultural responsibilities.

A tension that therefore comes to expression on the level of economic conduct exists between individuality and solidarity. Considerations of personal interests do not always and necessarily exhaust ethical desiderata or responsibility. The adage enters that one is, in ways that bear ethical reflection, his brother's keeper. In economic argument the implied criteria of solidarity call for address to the wider effects and potential reverberations that may follow individual decisions. There exists not only a macroeconomics to be set beside the atomistic analysis of microeconomic behavior. Considerations of macromorality also arise. That is so, at a minimum, on two levels.

First, individual action is necessarily action with relation to other participants in the economic production and exchange process. It is true that market action is what it is because of differences of valuations, utility expectations, preferences, and hopes on the part of market participants. It is hardly an adequate analytical assumption to posit that all market traders come to the exchange process with homogeneous expectations. Moreover, the bases of action provided by historical experience, awareness, interpretation, and the imagined grounds on which future possible outcomes may be contemplated understandably differ between individuals. But conceivably, certain canons of proper and ethical conduct inform production and exchange decisions. Questions of the presence or otherwise of honesty and integrity, the possibility or otherwise of market discrimination in the pursuit of profit, or the exploitation of concentrated market power exert their separate and unique ethical pressures.

Second, the issue of solidarity arises acutely in the consideration of the macroeconomic or society-wide implications of economic action and policy. That is so in at least two respects. In the first place, it is arguable that morality attaches to the attitudes that are taken to, and the policy programs that are recommended in connection with, the problem of unemployment and the underutilization of the economy's resources.

An economist might look out upon the world and be gratified that he or she sees 93 percent of the workforce employed. Another might look at the same data and see more prominently the seven percent unemployment. One might be dispositionally attached to the notion that a more or less freely functioning laissez faire market economy will ensure that all will work out for the best. By that means, it might be supposed, a high and generally satisfactory level of employment will be assured, and satisfactory levels of social and economic welfare will be realized as a result.

Another economist's attitude may be influenced by a greater concern for the relative deprivation and poverty that unemployment at any level entails. And for reasons of this kind, quite different views might be taken of the morality that is thought to attach to macrosocial outcomes. The economic policies that might be adapted to them will accordingly be variously evaluated. Considerations of prospective economic stability and growth, with their possible implications for inflationary disturbances, environmental spoliation, policy trade-offs, and intergenerational transfers will also be relevant.

At the same time, the question of solidarity comes to expression in relation to the realities of income and wealth distribution. That has to do with the view that is taken, and the morality issues that are deemed to be relevant, in relation to the economic endowments with which different individuals enter, or have an opportunity to enter, the economic and market process. On that level, also, questions arise of the possible redistribution of incomes that might be aimed to redress inequalities or inequities of wealth and resources. The conception of solidarity opens at that point the difficult question of the moral and ethical imperatives that might inform a wide range of possible welfare policies and programs.

Deontological and Consequentialist Ethical Criteria

The vocabulary we shall import from moral philosophy raises the highly significant divergence of attitudes that this dichotomy involves. It will anticipate the somewhat more technical summary in chapter 3 to observe no more than the essential meaning of the terms at this point.

Consequentialist ethical criteria look, for the justification or vindication of action, to the goodness or otherwise of the outcomes that might be judged to result from it. The contemplated consequences establish the propriety or rightness of the act. Such ethical desiderata have come to most forceful expression in economics in the long history of the influence of utilitarianism. The notion of cardinal utility, which was developed during the nineteenth century under the inspiration of the Benthamite calculus, gave way in due course to the neoclassical concepts of preference orderings and ordinal utility. But the concept of an implicit consequentialist justification of action survived, and it continued to exercise a dominance over the economic mind. It will be necessary, for that reason, to examine at some length the influence that utilitarianism has historically exercised in economics and to consider the justification of decisions and policies that it has been thought to entail.

On the other hand, deontological ethical criteria have regard, not to contemplated consequences, but to the sense of duty or obligation that lies behind action and behavior. In ethical theory, that sense of duty may be thought to be generated by any of a variety of causations. It will be clear, of course, that consequentialist and deontological criteria cannot always and necessarily be understood to be rigorously separable and distinct. One's sense of duty and obligation to an economic grouping, such as family or class or regional or national interests, may lead to actions and policy recommendations that contemplate objectives and ends that address primarily those interests.

It will be seen that an allegiance to grouping or class interests can quickly call in question the conventional emphasis of neoclassical theory on individualized or atomistic self-interest criteria. The point is eloquently argued, for example, in Sen's discussion of "Rational Fools" ([1976–77] 1979), where considerations of "sympathy" and "commitment" are invoked. Sen has "argued against viewing behaviour in terms of the traditional dichotomy between egoism and universalized moral systems (such as utilitarianism). Groups intermediate between oneself and all, such as class and community, provide the focus of many actions involving commitment" (109).

Further, the sharpness of the distinction between consequentialist and deontological criteria may be blurred for other reasons. It might be thought, for example, that a duty or obligation exists to do the will of God. But it might be envisioned at the same time that doing the will of God will in due course be rewarded in certain imaginable ways. To the extent that the contemplation of the latter gains an ascendancy in the determination of individuals' actions, a consequentialist element will have entered what was initially seen as a deontological motivation.

Entitlement and Contribution

In the discussion at a later point of the ethics and economics of welfare and wealth distribution, it will be suggested that considerations of social justice exert ethical imperatives. The literature on economic justice has recently expanded, and economists have been fairly heavily influenced by, for example, Rawls's well-known work on *A Theory of Justice* (1971). Its scope and emphases will be noted and an alternative suggestion will be made regarding the morality and ethics of systems and schemes of distribution. At that point, what will be referred to as an ethic of entitlement will be introduced.

But it is held to be of some importance that an ethic of contribution is correlative to that of entitlement. By contribution at that point is understood the deontological obligation to work or to contribute to the national production in which, by virtue of the ethic of entitlement, an individual has a right to share. That, in turn, raises at least two points that deserve minimal notice at this stage.

First, a wide range of possible schemes of entitlement, or bases of justification for economic redistributions, clearly exists. It follows that any statement that is made in support of one or the other will necessarily be influenced by personal and heavily individualized ethical and moral presuppositions. The immediate issue, therefore, is not any particular form or system of entitlement, but simply the notion that a correlativity is deemed to exist between the entitlement and the obligation of contribution as that has just been envisaged.

Second, it would be transparently misguided to speak of an ethic of contribution in this sense without at the same time recognizing that under certain circumstances the development of economic affairs may be such that there is no work for individuals to do. Economic fluctuations, and the possibility of more or less prolonged periods of economic depression, may render work opportunities less than readily available. It does not require an extensive reading of economic history to confirm this. Or again, technological advances may engender structural unemployment in certain skills or trades or regions. At that point, it might well be contemplated that ethical criteria attach to alternative possible economic policies that might be addressed to such a situation. Moral sensitivities, that is, might well be thought to be engaged in whatever macroeconomic policies and programs might be judged to be potentially effective in such situations.

In other words, the ethic of solidarity, or the ethic of concern for what are larger or more extensive than personalized and individualized self-interests, again comes to focus. That wider ethic also comes to confluence with what will be referred to in due course as questions of macromorality.

Static and Iterative Ethical Criteria

The concept of iteration is judged to be of singular importance in connection with the ethico-economic tensions that will be brought into view. The concept of iteration emanates from the reality that economic action and processes, and the outcomes, trends, and developments to which they give rise, occur in real historical time (I have discussed relevant issues at length in my *Economics and the Antagonism of Time*, 1994).

It is a well-established characteristic of received traditions in neoclassical economic analysis, as well as in modern reincarnations of the classical scheme of things, that time enters as only a logical or a serially-dated variable. I have discussed in other places both the timelessness of equilibrium theoretic systems in economics and what I have labeled the pseudotemporal dynamics of certain mathematically structured systems. Economic decisions and actions are necessarily made and taken in conditions of ignorance that are imposed by the sheer fact that the future is always unknowable. It is not merely the case that the future is unknown. It is, by virtue of the real time in which decision is bound, unknowable.

It is true that the economics discipline has invented ways and methods of analysis that are designed to abolish ignorance. The most prominent of these, which has been accorded extensive use in economic argument, is the probability calculus. But what is by now an extensive and expanding literature has cast serious doubts on the ready applicability of probability theorizing in economics (see references cited in Vickers 1994). To the extent that it is assumed that future possible outcomes can be corralled by probability assignments, or, that is, that the future values of specified variables can be described by assignable probability distributions, to that extent an assumption of knowledge is being made. But knowledge is the antithesis of ignorance, and to the extent that ignorance of the future is in that way assumed to be abolished, then for analytical purposes the future itself is also effectively abolished.

The impact of these considerations on our present discussion is that as time moves forward in its unidirectional trajectory, as economic conditions and structures and outcomes change, the need exists to reconsider the positions that are taken regarding the ethical justification of policies and actions. It is not possible, that is to say, to establish a once-and-for-all economic structure that satisfies, and that will automatically continue to satisfy, whatever ethical criteria and objectives are embraced. The ethical decision, with the need for ethical reevaluations, moves on. Ethical responsibility iterates in the context of what it is that the passing of real time bequeaths.

This point does not eliminate the possibility that the general nature of an ethical commitment in relation to economic affairs may itself be well established. Well-articulated ethical criteria may be held and assumedly satisfied. But in the nature of real time's forward movement, the highly important iterative component of ethical thought and prescription will require a continuing and iterative address to details of ethically acceptable policies and behavior. Changing assessment and reassessment of relevant economic criteria will be required. Schemes of income, wealth, and welfare distribution, for example, may continue to satisfy well-defined and generalized desiderata. But adjustments of degrees and ranges of entitlement, and of quantified benefits and obligations will undoubtedly need to be made. Time's unidirectional arrow too easily corrupts our best conceived plans and our judgments of detailed ethical justification.

Immanentistic and Transcendentalist Standpoints

In a larger and more extensively philosophic examination of ethical theory than it is our task to undertake, an issue of high importance has to do with the standpoint from which the very possibility and structure of ethical criteria are to be approached. In his influential *A Theory of Justice*, in which he set out his notions of "justice as fairness," his "difference principle," and "primary social goods," Rawls rightly referred to what is denominated the Archimedean point, or the standpoint from which ethical justifications are to be established. The terminology stems from the historic statement attributed to Archimedes when he said "Give me a point on which to stand and I will move the world." Or, as might be translated in other terms, give me a point on which I can stand in order to explain the world. Rawls is rightly concerned with the Archimedean point that establishes the character and flavor of ethical explanation.

The Archimedean point, in the fifth and final of our ethico-economic dichotomies, may be understood to be either immanentistic or transcendentalist. By transcendentalist is understood those bodies of theory whose starting point is taken to be, in some sense, extra-mundane. Such theories can be seen to point substantially to what have been referred to as deontological ethical criteria. Examples of transcendentalist theories are those whose categories of obligation emanate from a sense or assumption that canons of morality are supplied from a source outside of, rather than within, the world whose ethical justification is being sought. Kant's noumenal, as distinct from phenomenal, realm comes immediately to mind. But unlike Kant, for whom knowledge of the noumenal was, as he said, abolished in order to make room for faith, thinkers who build transcendentalist ethical systems appeal generally to a *sensus deitatis* and the assumption of the possibility of knowledge that flows from it. The obligation that is in such a way established or brought into view confirms the deontological character of the relevant thought scheme and its ethical content.

Immanentistic thought schemes, on the other hand, take their starting point from, and allow their criteria to be established in terms of, assumptions or categories that are intra-mundane. They set out to explain the world, that is, on the basis of postulates, or principles of the predication of meaning, that are grounded in realities discoverable within the world. The basis of explanation is thus discoverable within the explanandum itself.

We shall refer to what emerged as a prime example of an immanentistic-rationalist ethical criterion, namely that of Immanuel Kant whose categorical imperative has gained wide currency. Kant set out his categorical imperative in a form that implied what can be termed an absolutist ethic. On the level of normative ethical theory Kant's imperative claimed that one should "act only on that maxim through which you can at the same time will that it should become a universal law." Kant is here giving expression to two motifs that will engage us again: first, his notion of the autonomy of the individual, a conception that for him identified a central moral value (Kant [1785] 1948); and second, the notion of the universalizability of ethical criteria. The assumption of the autonomous knowing individual will be seen to spill over to influence the place of the individual in economic argument and to become triumphant, in a sense, in the highly individualized aspects of canonical neoclassical theory. The other question of the universalizability of ethical criteria will be seen to contain difficulties of implementation.

A FRAMEWORK OF ITERATIVE ACCOUNTABILITY AND SOLIDARITY

The five dichotomies within ethico-economic argument that we have discussed in skeletal fashion together provide the position or the standpoint from which the following ethical and economic analysis will proceed. To summarize, importance will be placed on the ethical significance of solidarity alongside that of individuality; recognition will be accorded deontological as distinct from consequentialist criteria; an ethic of obligation will be seen as correlative to that of entitlement; and emphasis will be placed on the iterative nature of economic developments and the attendant need for ethical reevaluations. At the same time, opportunity will be presented for reflection on the essentially immanentistic nature of certain modes of ethical presupposition.

These positions coalesce in what might be referred to as a *Framework of Iterative Accountability and Solidarity (FIAS)*. Individual and personal responsibility and accountability are seen, that is, as the bases of ethical desiderata and criteria. But that accountability extends also to the level of a solidaristic concern for the implications that actions and policies have for the social organism at large. Macroeconomic considerations, along with the implications for what will be referred to as macromorality, will accordingly be brought into view.

The *FIAS* framework as here articulated is not, however, intended to provide, and will not be used extensively to provide, an organon of enquiry in the sense that it is rigidly applicable in all of its parts to all situations. Rather, and more importantly, its several elements will be referred to as occasions and contexts warrant, and they will have varying and particular applications in differing ethico-economic situations. The important features of the framework are those that have been highlighted in the first paragraph of this section. A wide range of scope for their application will emerge.

The reference in the analysis that follows to the elements that have just been indicated will permit a consistent focus on both the ethical conceptions and the economic analysis that needs to be brought into view. It should be borne in mind that our present project, as indicated at the beginning, is concerned with what are seen as two highly interdependent and closely intermeshed issues and levels of argument. We are concerned both with the structure of ethical attitudes and analysis, and with the question of whether the ways in which the economy functions are best designed to meet the ethical criteria that are contemplated. We shall address as occasion warrants, that is, the related questions of how the economy works, what kinds of analytical explanation or economic theory are, or might be, brought to bear upon it, and the scope that might exist for the construction of new foundations on these various and interdependent levels.

PLAN OF THE BOOK

The examination of these and related themes is divided in the following chapters into two separate but closely related parts. First, the three chapters of part II are designed to provide a necessary background to the more detailed discussion of economic activity that follows. In chapter 2 a brief presentation is made of some aspects of the historical development of economic analysis, from the perspective of its relation with issues of ethical import. While no attempt has been made to present a complete or even a reasonably rounded review of the relevant intellectual history, the contributions of some of the principal architects of the economics discipline have been traced. It will be seen that in relation to the issues we shall bring under review, a number of those who were prominent in the formation of the neoclassical theory recanted from positions they had earlier taken.

In the second chapter of the background studies in part II, the structures of ethical theory are addressed in a summary and nontechnical fashion, and some relevant parts of the vocabulary and the concept formation of ethical theory are clarified. The distinction will be drawn between the discussion of meta-ethics and the statement of normative ethical criteria. The final chapter of part II raises the question as to whether economics is, or can be, or should be, a value-free enquiry. While that question has been extensively answered in the affirmative by received traditions, an alternative viewpoint will be presented. The discussion in chapter 4 will expand on the preliminary historical review in chapter 2 and will trace the contributions and the results of some of the relevant debates during the nineteenth century.

In the four chapters of part III the analysis moves to a direct discussion of points at which, in relation to economic theory and policy, questions of ethical criteria arise. At the same time, new ways of looking at the structures of economic argument will be proposed at appropriate points. In chapters 5 and 6 a number of issues that raise scope for ethical judgment in relation to market activity are discussed, taking account of actions and decisions on both the supply and the demand sides of the market. Marginal valuations, for example marginal productivity and marginal utility, will come under inspection, as will the important question of income and wealth distribution. The ethical content of schemes of distribution that have been proposed will be examined.

The concluding chapter 8 takes up issues of macroeconomics and macromorality. It is argued there that doubt can be cast on the logical and the ethical sufficiency of the claim that the macroeconomy can be left to settle automatically at a position of full employment, or at a natural rate of unemployment. Ethical concern is raised by the existence and condition of the unemployed and those that suffer from the malfunctioning of the market and economic system. Raised in that context is the question of distributive justice, and an alternative to Rawls's well-known difference principle is proposed. Economic policies that are calculated to keep the economy on an even keel and growing at a maintainable rate will be briefly reviewed, and in that connection a conception of collective macromorality will inform our concluding argument.

Part II
The Status of Economic and Ethical Theory

2 ECONOMICS AND THE DISSOLUTION OF THE ETHICAL IDEAL

The philosopher-economists who, in the context of the crumbling social cohesion of the later Middle Ages, produced the beginnings of systematic economic thought were primarily concerned to lay down systems of moral axioms. Their objective, in essence, was to defend the cultural status quo against the encroachment of the market system. Thomas Aquinas (1225–1274) and his teacher Albertus Magnus (1193–1280) (see Schumpeter 1954, chap. 3), argued eloquently to that end, though Aquinas had much that is interesting to say regarding usury or the rate of interest, the just price, and the justification of private property. But the demands of economic and social justice, as they were understood to be served by the preservation of the status quo, were elevated to prior concern. In that early scheme of things, morality mattered (see Dempsey [1935] 1960).

But the priority of that concern evaporated. We shall review in this chapter some of the principal highlights of the devolution that occurred.

EARLY ECONOMIC ANALYSIS

In the high days of mercantilism both the writers and the writing in economics were markedly changed. Now the businessman, the trader, the self-interested capitalist and profiteer replaced the university men, the philosophers and theologians and moralizers, who had earlier commanded the field. Mun (1571–1641), Misselden (1608–1654), Child (1630–1699), and Gee (fl.1725–1750) are representative authors. They were followed, in the later mercantilism of the seventeenth and eighteenth centuries, by authors who produced substantial treatises on aspects of economic activity and analysis. Those of Locke (1691), Cantillon (1734), Hume (1752), and Steuart (1767), along with those of the physiocrats Quesnay (1759), are the principal forerunners of Adam Smith's *An Inquiry into the Nature and Causes of the Wealth of Nations* ([1776] 1937). Their technical contributions and their significance for the history of economic thought have been evaluated in other places (Vickers 1959; 1975; 1995).

In that earlier age of pamphleteering that Schumpeter refers to as "prescientific" (1954, 9, 143), the contributions to economic argument were contained mainly in essays directed to specific points of traders' economic self-interest. An earlier dimension of ethical presupposition had lapsed. Exceptions to that general development did, of course, occur. Between the Renaissance and the Reformation at one end of the modern period and the gathering pace, at the other end, of eighteenth- and nineteenth-century industrialization, a concern for the ethical substratum of economic argument did come to expression. Weber ([1904–5] 1958), Tawney (1926), Samuelsson (1957), Robertson ([1933] 1959), and others have produced a well-known and widely-cited literature that bears on the point.

Evaluative perspectives on this period of intellectual history have varied. Jacob Viner, the distinguished mid-twentieth-century economist, has addressed the principal thrust of "eighteenth-century ethics . . . [that] concerned itself with man's behavior in society. . . . In whatever senses it may be true that eighteenth-century thought was 'individualistic,' it was not true in the sense that any important writers of the century failed to stress obligations of the individual to his community as a central datum . . . of morality" (1972, 59). Viner's suggestion here of the communitarian concern of the eighteenth-century authors anticipates a motif to which we have already referred, that of the tension between individuality and solidarity in ethical criteria.

In his critical evaluation of the period under review, Viner is taking issue with Tawney's "prolonged campaign to persuade us that the age of capitalism was marked by a deterioration of the social ethics of the western world as compared with the age of serfdom" (59). From this Viner-Tawney debate, Viner's conclusion is sustainable that "there is no logical conflict between a socially oriented teleology and individualism if the individual either has conscious social ends or by providential design serves such ends without having adopted them as his own ultimate objective" (60). It is precisely such a relation, a conception, as Walsh sees it, of a "Divine Plan," that was affirmed in Adam Smith's "hidden hand" (see Walsh 1987, 3:865–66) or that is implicit in Viner's conception of "providence" (1972; see also Viner 1978).

Granted that issues of economic morality did in this way emerge again or provide something of an undercurrent to economic argument, two aspects of the early classical and the nineteenth-century developments can be noted. First, in the definitive economics treatise that laid the foundations for the classical system, in Adam Smith's work for example, a sensitivity to ethical proprieties again entered the universe of discourse. That is so even if, as it has to be seen in retrospect, it occurred in a shadowy or less than fully satisfactory sense. Second, the development of economic thought in the nineteenth century was such that the relevance of ethical proprieties was again in due course submerged. The intellectual movement of the times was to the elevation of the "rational economic man," the fictional character, materialistic, omniscient, extremum-seeking, acquisitive, and substantially hedonistic, who became, in the wider social consciousness, the most recognizable feature of the economics discipline.

The classical economic analysis that matured from its early nineteenth-century beginnings in the hands of James Mill, Ricardo, Malthus, Senior, Say, and Chalmers passed its bequest of a severe a priori deductivism to the later neoclassicism. In the course of its doing so, a number of distinctive strands of thought emerged. Joseph Schumpeter, one of the last to command a comprehensive view of the history of the subject, has etched the cultural and intellectual features of the period. In his reference to the "mental furniture" of the age, Schumpeter had in view "the *Weltanschaung* of laicist liberalism," a "utilitarian ethics," and what he saw as the philosophy of "an evolutionary rather than mechanistic materialism" (1954, 772). Max Weber, who had earlier produced his essay on " 'Objectivity' in Social Science and Social Policy" (in 1949), understood the subject to have been "from the very beginning . . . integrated into the great scheme of the natural law and rationalistic *Weltanschaung* of the eighteenth century . . . with its optimistic faith in the theoretical and practical rationalizability of reality" (Hausman 1984, 107).

An important aspect of Weber's approach to what he referred to as one of the "cultural sciences" was his insistence on the importance of the "presuppositions" with which one "approaches his subject matter" in the attempt to "discover what is meaningful to us" (Hausman 1984, 101, 102, 104). That presuppositional content of economic reasoning comes to focus in the evaluation of the possibility of economics as a value-free discipline.

THE NINETEENTH CENTURY

These observations and Schumpeter's analysis of the cultural climate in which economics came to maturity provoke at least a brief reflection on some threads of historical connection. The "laicist liberalism" to which Schumpeter referred fostered, as popular imagination has understood it, the laissez faire that characterized the classical system (Schumpeter 1954, 773). But by the later nineteenth century the confidence in laissez faire liberalism that had been abroad in headier days had come under increasing stress, if not shown signs of crumbling. Keynes, for example, raised the issue in his essay on "The End of Laissez-faire" in 1926, some ten years before he published the *General Theory*.

Let us clear from the ground the metaphysical or general principles upon which, from time to time, *laissez faire* has been founded. It is *not* true that individuals possess a prescriptive "natural liberty" in their economic activities. There is *no* "compact" conferring perpetual rights on those who Have or on those who Acquire. The world is *not* so governed from above that private and social interests always coincide. It is *not* so managed here below that in practice they coincide. It is *not* a correct deduction from the principles of economics that enlightened self-interest always operates in the public interest. Nor is it true that self-interest generally is enlightened; more often individuals acting separately to promote their own ends are too ignorant or too weak to attain even these. Experience does *not* show that individuals, when they make up a social unit, are always less clear-sighted than when they act separately. ([1931] 1972, 9:287–88)

It is not intended or necessary to commit our discussion to all of what might be implied in, or inferred from, this statement of Keynes. But against the concept of the freedom of economic movement that the notion of laissez faire fostered, a number of tensions mounted in economic thought as the classical system matured. Of foremost relevance is the tension we have referred to as that between individuality or individualism on the one hand and solidarity on the other. The laicization of thought had by that time influenced heavily also the culturally determinative significance of religion, whose erstwhile hegemony had contributed to societal and behavioral moorings. Religion was fading from the social consciousness. Or perhaps it was the case that as religion was laicized to an increasing extent, it gave rise to a faltering of beliefs at the same time as it formed a veneer over the mores of Victorian optimism and its still extensive ecclesiasticism.

The religious and political Reformation and what followed from it from the sixteenth to the nineteenth century, whose influence Weber ([1904–5] 1958) and Tawney (1926) explored at length, had led to an emphasis on individualism, as that derived from the Reformation's rediscovery of the sanctity and worth of the individual. Along with that, as has already been observed, the cultural conviction of solidarity, or the conception that one was in some sense his brother's keeper, had remained alive. Considerations of societal or group allegiances and responsibility influenced to varying degrees the proprieties of individual action. That important conception was no doubt reinforced by a number of intellectual movements in the mid-nineteenth century. They included the socialist dissent, the challenge to new awarenesses that Marx had raised, the midcentury movement of Christian Socialism and its explicit economic claims, and the literature of social criticism which, in the hands of Dickens for example, disturbed the social conscience. There did emerge at that time a specifically laicized movement, instanced, for example, in the work of Wilberforce (inspired by the erstwhile slave trader turned evangelist, John Newton) and Shaftesbury, that made significant contributions to the amelioration of social and economic conditions.

But the tensions mounted, tensions between individuality and solidarity as they generated or implied behavior criteria and optimal social constructs; between a scientistic-positivist methodological presupposition and a distinctively economic way of seeing things in social science discourse; between what came to be referred to as the normative and the positive in economics; and between the substantive and the ethical in economic argument and presupposition. As opinion was determined by a climate of progress and the pushing back of scientific, economic, and geographical frontiers, it came increasingly under the influence of the methodological bequest of the natural sciences, the expandingly confident expressions of social Darwinism, and the newer emphases on positivism in sociology and philosophy. That was, as will be observed immediately, markedly true in the case of the opinion leaders that provided the principal formative influences in economics.

But as these tensions mounted, the ethical principles that inhered in earlier philosophic commitments did in some muted sense remain, or at least on the surface of things they claimed some confessional allegiance. As Schumpeter has observed, Alfred Marshall (1842–1924), who was a principal architect of English language neoclassicism, began his career and intellectual journey with a commitment to the theology of the Church of England, though that was in due course discarded. But Marshall, as did the generalized culture of the time, "preserved the ethical inheritance of Christianity and was in general not actively hostile to the abandoned beliefs and to the churches that taught them" (1954, 772). Of course the rejoinder can be made to that conclusion that the unfortunate and damaging assumption of the time was that the Christian ethic was supportable without the Christian doctrine. When the latter had been effectively scuttled, the former became rootless, no longer securely moored, and without a meaningful rationale.

The issue of such a commitment as Schumpeter has attributed to Marshall is raised because it stands, in the history of cultural and intellectual development, as one of the significant explanatory factors that has caused the bequest of the nineteenth to the twentieth century to be what it was. Economics, as the discipline matured from the nineteenth-century neoclassicism onward, set out to establish a value-free or, as it imagined, a scientific enquiry. It separated the normative from the positive, a methodological stance that was heavily influenced by John Neville Keynes's *Scope and Method of Political Economy* (1891). A history of the distinction we have in view is presented by Hutchison in characteristically insightful fashion in his *'Positive' Economics and Policy Objectives* (1964, 23–50).

In making that distinction, economics brought to articulate expression the assumptions of the rational economic man, a fictional being fathered by the Kantian assumption of the autonomous individual. That critical assumption of autonomy, moreover, influenced most of what emerged as economic analysis in the century that followed. It projected on the ethico-philosophic level a tension of which the economics discipline has remained substantially unaware. That has to do with the relation, paradoxical to a degree, between the notion of self-interested individualism on the one hand and, on the other, that of the universalizability of behavioral laws or criteria.

That notion of universalizability was embedded in Kant's categorical imperative. In him there culminates the entailment of the anthropocentricity that Descartes had stood for at the beginning of the modern period. The bold and the culturally absorbing sweep of what came to be known in the next three hundred years as modernism, with its bequest to economics of the individualized economic man, has only lately begun to crumble. It has been challenged in more recent times by newer forms of so-called postmodernism, whose thought schemes have replaced the notion of the autonomous economic man by the "socially constituted" participant in the economic process.

But from the eighteenth-century Enlightenment that Kant culminated, through the laissez faire assumptions that it nurtured, the nascent economics discipline turned for its explanatory principles to its famous and familiar rational economic man. That invention was accompanied by a widening theological Arminianism that also projected, from its unique level of influence, the assumptions of the autonomy of the individual. The norms and influence of the rational economic man were projected into virtually all of the economic thought that ensued. That exogenously structured individual stood for all the demands of individuality and the congealing philosophy of individualism. As the economic theorists saw him, he encapsuled in his being and behavior all that the pervasive assumptions of methodological individualism connoted. He came to the marketplace with assumedly well-defined endowments, resources, skills, abilities, technologies, preferences, and tastes, and was untouched by the forces of social movement that swirled around him. The rational economic man was not in any sense constituted by the market process in which he participated. He was exogenous from it, autonomous, and in him the Kantian and the Enlightenment assumptions of individual autonomy were apotheosized. The anthropocentric postulate with which the Cartesian rationalism gave birth to modern philosophy had sired its offspring in the rational economic man.

Kant, of course, whose influence we shall see in a moment extended explicitly to Marshall in the neoclassical period, was no doubt more sensitive than Smith to the darker potentialities of people and their economic behavior. For him, it was the individual's supposed subscription to the ethical categorical imperative (which, as we have seen, implied the universalizability of the behavior criteria) that led potentially to socially responsible or acceptable action and outcomes. The latter did not depend, for him, on the same beneficent unintended consequences to which Smith in general held. Indeed, Kant's vision of society rested on his conception of antagonism as the cause of human progress. In that connection he proposed his well-known analogy of the forest where the competition of the trees for air and sunlight contributed to their growth (Kant 1991, 46). Without that competition the trees would grow feeble, and similarly, without antagonisms, society would tend to a simple, Arcadian, pastoral life.

It is relevant to our preliminary observations on the trends in economic thought and perspectives in the nineteenth century to take note of Keynes's summing up, as contained in a perceptive paragraph from his biographical essay on Marshall.

Marshall's Cambridge career came just at the date which will, I think, be regarded by the historians of opinion as the critical moment at which Christian dogma fell away from the serious philosophical world of England, or at any rate of Cambridge. In 1863 Henry Sidgwick, aged twenty-four, had subscribed to the Thirty-Nine Articles [of the Church of England] as a condition of tenure of his Fellowship, and was occupied in reading Deuteronomy in Hebrew and preparing lectures on the Acts of the Apostles. Mill, the greatest intellectual influence on the youth of the age, had written nothing which clearly indicated any divergence from received religious opinions up to his *Examination of Hamilton* in 1865. At about this time Leslie Stephen was an Anglican clergyman, James Ward a Nonconformist minister, Alfred Marshall a candidate for holy orders, W.K. Clifford a High Churchman. In 1869 Sidgwick resigned his Trinity Fellowship, "to free myself from dogmatic obligations." A little later none of these could have been called Christians. Nevertheless, Marshall, like Sidgwick, was as far as possible from adopting an "anti-religious" attitude. He sympathized with Christian morals and Christian ideals and Christian incentives. There is nothing in his writings depreciating religion in any form; few of his pupils could have spoken definitely about his religious opinions. At the end of his life he said, "Religion seems to me an attitude," and that, though he had given up Theology, he believed more and more in Religion. The great change-over of the later sixties was an intellectual change, not the ethical or emotional change which belongs to a later generation, and it was a wholly intellectual debate which brought it about. (1956, 44ff.)

Much has been made in the history of economics of the influence on Marshall of Henry Sidgwick, the philosopher-economist to whom Keynes has just referred, and whom the American philosopher Rescher described as a "subtle and profound utilitarian" (Rescher 1966, x. See Sidgwick [1874] 1962; Schneewind 1977). Marshall said of Sidgwick that "I was fashioned by him. He was so to speak my spiritual father and mother" (Hutchison, 1953, 51). On the other hand, Marshall's earlier interest in philosophy had taken him to Germany and to a study of Kant, whom he referred to as "Kant my guide, the only man I ever worshipped" (Keynes 1956, 48). The roots of Kantian autonomy in this way came to flower in the English language neoclassical economics, though there is no reason to believe that such an explicit Kantian influence was exerted on the economists of the period in general.

An interesting light on the earlier climate of opinion is thrown also by Munby in a highly informative study. He has pointed out that in the period we have under review "in the university of those days, elections to Chairs were dependent on theological rectitude rather than on any contribution to learning" (1963, 81. See also T.S. Eliot 1940, to whose work Munby's is a rejoinder). Munby reports an interesting situation in which in 1836 F.D. Maurice (an ancestor of the distinguished twentieth-century economist, Joan Robinson) agreed to stand for election to the Chair of Political Economy at Oxford on the ground that there appeared to be no one else ready to stand with the support of a theological party, and on the ground that "political economy is not the foundation of morals and politics, but must have them for its foundation or be worth nothing." Maurice, it is reported, knew nothing of political economy but was prepared to "endeavour to master the details of the subject." But in the outcome, the support of the Tractarians was withdrawn from him and he did not accede to the chair (Munby 1963, 81).

A final perspective on what had developed in the pre-twentieth century period is provided by an argument of Adam Smith, the oft-claimed parent of academic economics. We are indebted to James Bonar's *Philosophy and Political Economy* for preserving a significant but little known section of the first edition of Smith's *Theory of Moral Sentiments*. Smith had published that work a couple of decades before his more widely known *Wealth of Nations*, and controversy has ensued regarding the possible grounds on which Smith's seemingly different positions in the two separate works should be harmonized (see V. Brown 1991). It is to the *Moral Sentiments* that we can look for a closer view of the ethics behind the economic position of Smith, who had held the Chair of Logic and subsequently the Chair of Moral Philosophy at Glasgow University. In his earlier work he had examined the cohesiveness of human society and had emphasized the concept of sympathy as a cementing element. In his work on morals, Skinner has concluded, Smith "argued that all men possess by nature certain faculties and propensities, such as reason, imagination, and *fellow-feeling*, on whose exercise moral judgment depends" (1975, 3, italics added). Those assumptions, moreover, retained a discoverable influence over Smith's subsequent work.

But the notions that had been explicit in the *Moral Sentiments* slip into the background or, it may be argued, remain implicit in the *Wealth of Nations*, where the functioning of the market undergoes extensive scrutiny.

The following comment, which was omitted from all editions of the *Moral Sentiments* subsequent to the first, is a counterpoint to what, on the basis of the mainstream of Smith's work and his principal bequest to economics, might be regarded as his optimistic humanist and individualist philosophy. Smith is here discussing the nature and meaning of virtue and vice, and he adopts a standpoint which, it will be clear, is as much concerned with the Hebrew concept of sin as with the Greek concept of vice.

If we consult our natural sentiments, we are apt to fear lest before the holiness of God, vice should appear to be more worthy of punishment than the weakness and imperfections of human virtue can ever seem to be of reward. Man when about to appear before a being of infinite perfection can feel but little confidence in his own merit or in the imperfect propriety of his own conduct. . . . If he would still hope for happiness, he is conscious that he cannot demand it from the justice, but that he must entreat it from the mercy of God. Repentance, sorrow, humiliation, contrition at the thought of his past conduct are, upon this account, the sentiments that become him, and seem to be the only means which he has left for appeasing that wrath which, he knows, he has justly provoked. . . . Some other intercession, some other sacrifice, some other atonement, he imagines, must be made for him beyond what he himself is capable of making, before the purity of Divine justice can be reconciled to his manifold offences. . . . (Bonar 1893, 182-83)

Bonar, sometime lecturer in economics in the University Extension Movement in London, and in the early decades of this century Deputy Master of the Royal Mint in Ottawa, is here writing against the background of his extensive scholarship in classical economics. He is justly renowned for his definitive biography of Malthus ([1885] 1924) as well as for his work on Smith and Ricardo. The Smith he reveals in the extract from the *Moral Sentiments* that we have quoted is not, of course, the Smith that has come down through the history of thought, nor the Smith with which contemporary economics has substantial familiarity.

The point that has been raised, however, does alert us to the several ways in which Smith did entertain doubts as to the moral and ethical robustness of participants in the economic process. In the context in his *Wealth of Nations* of his discussion of the "education of youth" he observed that "such, it seems, is the natural insolence of man, that he almost always disdains to use the good instrument, except when he cannot or dare not use the bad one" ([1776] 1937, 751). And he acknowledged the potential disadvantages that accrued from differences in industrial power centers in his observation that

masters are always and every where in a sort of tacit, but constant and uniform combination, not to raise the wages of labour above their natural rate . . . Masters too sometimes enter into particular combinations to sink the wages of labour below this rate. ([1776] 1937, 66–67)

Smith again takes up the theme:

Our merchants and master-manufacturers complain much of the bad effects of high wages in raising the price, and thereby lessening the sale of their goods both at home and abroad. They say nothing concerning the bad effects of high profits. They are silent with regard to the pernicious effects of their own gains. They complain only of those of other people. ([1776] 1937, 98)

"People of the same trade seldom meet together," Smith observed, "even for merriment and diversion, but the conversation ends in a conspiracy against the public, or in some contrivance to raise prices" ([1776] 1937, 128). He concluded that

the interest of the dealers, however, in any particular branch of trade or manufactures, is always in some respects different from, and even opposite to, that of the public. [The dealers are] an order of men, whose interest is never exactly the same with that of the public, who have generally an interest to deceive and even to oppress the public, and who accordingly have, upon many occasions, both deceived and oppressed it. ([1776] 1937, 250)

Writing in *The New Palgrave: A Dictionary of Economics*, Vivian Walsh has addressed this important set of questions regarding Adam Smith's philosophic and ethical positions and the relation between Smith's two separate works, the *Moral Sentiments* and the *Wealth of Nations*. Walsh rightly draws attention to the conception of the "Divine Plan" that underlies Smith's vision of the working of the "invisible hand" ([1776] 1937, 423) and the unintended consequences of economic and market activity. Walsh suggests, not inappropriately, that contemporary analytical economists "would presumably not wish to be saddled with belief in [Smith's] Divine Plan" (1987, 3:866). Cognate issues are explored in Raphael's discussion of Smith's notion of "The Impartial Spectator" in the context of his moral philosophy (Raphael 1975, 83–99). One judges the morality or the ethical content of his own actions, that is, by considering how they would appear to an impartial spectator. That spectator may, in turn, be individual conscience.

TWENTIETH-CENTURY REACTION AND DEVELOPMENTS

The bequest to subsequent economic thought of the trends that developed throughout the nineteenth century raises a number of issues of immediate relevance. Edwin Seligman, a scholar of wide erudition and the occupant of the McVickar professorship of political economy at Columbia University in the early twentieth century, has examined the "materialistic" or, as he preferred, the "economic interpretation of history" (1907. See also

Schumpeter [1934] 1961, 57ff.). In doing so, he raises again and opens for ongoing discussion a methodological issue that comes into contact with those we have already raised. Let it be conceded, Seligman observes, "that the history of mankind is the history of man in society, and therefore social history in its broadest sense." He goes on to argue that

the question has arisen as to the fundamental causes of this social development— the reason of these great changes in human thought and human life which form the conditions of progress. No more profound and far-reaching question can occupy our attention; for upon the correct answer depends our whole attitude [note again the appearance of the Marshall-Keynes terminology] toward life itself. (1907, 2)

Seligman acknowledges that the economic category established by the thesis he examines fails to provide of itself significant explanatory results. He quotes with approval the early summing up of Simonde de Sismondi in 1819 that accused the orthodox school of "forgetting the men for the things; of sacrificing the end to the means." Seligman sees the orthodox scheme as "producing a beautiful logic, but a total forgetfulness of man and human nature" (1925, 15). "From the purely philosophical standpoint," he concludes,

it may be confessed that the theory, especially in its extreme form, is no longer tenable as the universal explanation of all human life. No monistic interpretation of humanity is possible. . . . As a philosophical doctrine of universal validity, the theory of "historical materialism" can no longer be successfully defended. (1907, 159)

But the rejection in this fashion of any "monistic interpretation" calls sharply into question the attempt to explain economic affairs by dislodging them from an underlying ethical commitment.

To reach into the field of literature and social commentary for a moment and to note its contiguity with the economic question, the British poet and essayist, T.S. Eliot, has addressed similar propositions in his work on *The Idea of a Christian Society*. In that he is "concerned with . . . the organization of values, and a direction of religious thought which must inevitably proceed to a criticism of political and economic systems" (1940, vii). He quotes with approval the proposition that

men have lived by *spiritual* institutions (of some kind) in every society, and also by *political* institutions and, indubitably, by *economic* activities. Admittedly, they have, at different periods, tended to put their trust mainly in one of the three as the real cement of society, but at no time have they wholly excluded the others, because it is impossible to do so. (1940, vi, italics added)

The critical question, of course, relates to the nature of the coordinating rubric under which one's categories of social evaluation are themselves brought into harmony and to mutual interdependence. Kenneth Boulding, the prominent British-American economist in the mid-twentieth century, put the matter of ethico-economic interrelationship pointedly in his observation that "at the policy level, economics without ethics is a lever without a fulcrum" (1958, vi). But it is difficult to share Boulding's despair and agnosticism, which reflects the agnosticism that we shall see Joan Robinson advanced, when he concludes, in his response to the problem of what determines "the dominant value system" in society, that "this is a question to which at the present time there seems to be no good answers" (1958, 428).

John Maynard Keynes, from whose summary of the flavor of the nineteenth-century thought we have quoted, has given us no reason to believe that his own intellectual and professional position was touched by the Christian ethical grounding from which he understood the predecessor architects of his discipline to have recanted. He recorded in his memoirs, in his essay on *My Early Beliefs*, the priority of the influence upon him of the philosophy of Moore.

We accepted Moore's religion, so to speak, and discarded his morals. Indeed, in our opinion, one of the greatest advantages of his religion, was that it made morals unnecessary—meaning by 'religion' one's attitude [note that the concept of "attitude" had been earlier employed by Marshall in his summing up of his position] towards oneself and the ultimate and by "morals" one's attitude towards the outside world and the intermediate. . . . There was not a very intimate connection between "being good" and "doing good." (1956, 242–43)

Keynes in due course observed that "I see no reason to shift from the fundamental intuitions of [Moore's] *Principia Ethica*; though they are much too few and too narrow to fit actual experience . . . " (1956, 250). He went on to acknowledge that his "pseudo-rational view of human nature led to a thinness, a superficiality, not only of judgement, but also of feeling" (1956, 254).

The sketch we have drawn to this point, however, in no sense provides a complete examination of the philosophical and ethical stance that came to characterize the economists' positions. But in summary it can be said that as their academic and social impact developed into the twentieth century, a broader methodological and ethical characterization was warranted. In general, it can be said that economics was consolidated in the metaphysical assumptions of the autonomy of man, specifically the economic man and more generally the individual in his or her epistemic and ethical capacities. It became preoccupied with the construction of a tidily logical, quasi-mathematical, self-contained system of thought, positivistic and sanitized from ethical encumbrances, that is only now showing signs of stirring from its self-imposed shackles of supposed ethical neutrality.

A commentary on the state of affairs that has been reached in the discipline is provided by the concluding pages of the *Economic Philosophy* of Joan Robinson. Addressing finally the moral problem that surrounds economic thought and policy, Joan Robinson offered only a darkened and discouraging agnosticism:

The moral problem is a conflict that can never be settled. Social life will always present mankind with a choice of evils. No metaphysical solution that can ever be formulated will seem satisfactory for long. The solutions offered by economists were no less delusory than those of the theologians that they displaced. All the same we must not abandon . . . hope. . . . It is necessary to clear the decaying remnants of obsolete metaphysics out of the way before we can go forward. (1962, 146)

Joan Robinson's "obsolete metaphysics" will not be our principal concern. But the implications that they and their successor thought systems projected to the economics discipline will engage us in the following chapters.

CONTEMPORARY CONSTRUCTIONS

It is sufficient to cull from the foregoing that, as Rothschild has summarized it in his recent study, "ethics and economics have a long common past" (1993, 15). We have observed that two centuries ago, as mercantilism gave way in the eighteenth century to deeper social and economic thought, the ethical provided a substratum of awareness beneath the nascent and technical economic analytics. We have seen the intertwined expression of ethics and economics in Adam Smith's seminal works. It would be some time before that amalgam would be fairly definitively dissolved. But the dissolution of the ethical ideal did come, and the beginning of its decline, and what was to become its rather hurried demise, can be traced to the high and heady days of the classical economics in the early decades of the nineteenth century.

The general nature of contemporary constructions can be appreciated by taking note of the foci around which that devolution turns. David Ricardo ([1817] 1911) stands at one end and Leon Walras ([1874] 1969) at the other. By that it is meant, first, that the methodological revolution that Ricardo accomplished effectively extruded the ethical from the ethico-economic discourse that occupied the times; and second, that in Walras, or now in the widely current forms of the neo-Walrasian equilibrium theoretic revival, economic analysis has become almost exclusively a matter of mathematical technique, effectively divorced entirely from its erstwhile ethical presuppositions. Sen is on sound ground in observing that Walras the engineer gave impetus to what Sen has referred to as the "engineering" or the "logistic" approach, rather than the "ethics-related" approach to the development of economics (Sen 1987, 4–5).

Ricardo, as is well known, introduced into the discipline a rigorous a priori deductivism. It was imagined that all that economics was able to contribute to social discourse could be deduced from a fairly circumscribed set of basic postulates or assumptions descriptive of human behavior. Adam Smith, as to his analytical method, had presented in his *Wealth of Nations* a judicious mixture of historical information, real world description and illustrative arguments, along with deductions regarding market participants' behavior. He explored in that manner the consequent movements towards, as he referred to it, the "wealth of nations." But Ricardo changed that. There exists a highly informative exchange of letters between Ricardo and Malthus in which Ricardo insisted that sound reasoning in economics should concentrate on the longer-run outcomes of possible changes in economic assumptions or inputs. "One great cause of our difference," Ricardo observed to Malthus,

is that you have always in your mind the . . . temporary effects of particular changes—whereas I . . . fix my whole attention on the permanent state of things which will result from them. (1951–73, 7:120, quoted in Milgate, 1982, 56)

The difference of methodology between the Reverend Malthus and the stockbroker-speculator Ricardo (of Jewish faith, who married a Quaker and converted to Christianity) is highly informative. For it is in the immediate, short run, and impact situations and conditions that the ethical imperatives and their adjudicating relevance in economics come most forcibly to expression. In Ricardo's methodological deductivism, however, and in his severe a priorism that has continued to inform analytical economics into this century, the way was opened to the attempted construction of a distinctively value-free discipline.

The Walrasian general equilibrium theoretic system, certainly in its contemporary reincarnation, stands as the end result of the fact that the nascent economic thought schemes were shunted onto that supposedly ethically neutral road. The Walrasian scheme rests its analytical propositions on what we have observed as the presuppositions of the autonomous, rational economic individual. It understands market participants, on both the demand and the supply sides, to come to their production and exchange decisions with prespecified endowments of resources, skills, tastes, technologies, knowledges, and preferences, leaving none of those characteristics to be influenced or determined by the production and exchange process itself. The economic problem, as it is seen from that point onwards, is effectively that of finding the equilibrium solution values of vectors of outcome variables that define the mutual equilibration of all of the interdependent markets in the system.

Inherent in what has developed as the contemporary neo-Walrasian apparatus is the implication that, as it has been put, "human relationships in economics [are] represented as if they were relationships among inputs and outputs . . . relationships among things, not people" (Bowles and Gintis 1993, 4). That judgment recalls the complaint that Seligman had already registered. That, finally, is the magnificent Walrasian fiction, a grander fiction even than that of the famous auctioneer that operated Walras' tâtonnement market equilibration procedure.

There is thus within the Walrasian multi-market, mutually equilibrating system little room, not only for the individual who is replaced by his supply and demand functions, but also for the business firm that operates ubiquitously in the economic arena. Instead of the firm there is simply a combination of factors of production that come together to make outputs and a consequent juxtaposition of outputs and the utility-maximizing demands for them. It is those juxtapositions that are accorded the nomenclature of markets. Production functions on the one side come into symbiotic relations with utility functions on the other, and the genuine scope for individual decision and action, or for the ethical transliteration of their meaning, is abolished by the dictatorship of formalized maximization rules.

It is no doubt true that similar procedures of mathematization and assumptions of harmonious equilibration informed other intellectual disciplines as they matured during the nineteenth century. The development of the natural sciences, including biology, may be profitably investigated from that perspective. But it in no sense follows that the same methodology and investigative procedures are readily or efficiently importable into economics. In the latter, the objects of investigation are the outcomes of deliberate behavior by sentient, acting, reacting, and motivated individuals. They can be understood to provide explanations of why their decisions and actions are what they are. But it would strain credulity to imagine an explanation from the things and objects of the natural sciences as to why, for example, the attraction between them was related to the square of the distance separating them. Not only on the level of ethics that is our present concern, but on the level of epistemology and the construction of knowledge in general, it will be necessary to ask again whether a parity exists between the natural and the social sciences.

Between the deductivism of Ricardo at one end and the mathematized neo-Walrasianism at the other, economics set out to develop a system of enquiry that was purportedly ethically neutral. It aped the laws and development of the natural sciences. In the same way as the latter discovered the laws of natural systems, economics set out to discover and formulate the laws of social behavior and development. Marx, of course, was, on another level, a foremost practitioner in that endeavor. As in the natural realm, so now in the economic and the social, the establishment of a pure science was the objective. That pure science was addressed, in the case of economics, to the explanation of the criteria of the optimum choice of means to achieve specified ends. But for the economist, the ends were reckoned to be given and prespecified. The economist, qua economist, was not reckoned to be concerned with the goodness or the badness of the ends. If he were, then his scientific activity would inevitably be ethically tainted. To recall an earlier characterization, economics needed to develop as a severely positive science. The normative needed to be kept religiously separate and distinct. Positivism rode high (see Hutchison 1964).

The starkest demarcation of the ethical from the economic, the highwater mark or the articulate distillation of that distinctive methodology, occurred explicitly in Lionel Robbins's classic and *influential Essay on the Nature and Significance of Economic Science* ([1935] 1948). After setting down his definition of economics as "the science which studies human behaviour as a relationship between ends and scarce means which have alternative uses" (16), Robbins went on to confront directly the question of ethics and its place in relation to economic enquiry. His argument is worthy of fuller inspection in the context of our present study.

Economics is neutral as between ends. Economics cannot pronounce on the validity of ultimate judgments of value. . . . In recent years certain economists, realising this inability of Economics, thus conceived, to provide within itself a series of principles binding upon practice, have urged that the boundaries of the subject should be extended to include normative studies . . . [but] economics deals with ascertainable facts; ethics with valuations and obligations. . . . Between the generalisations of positive and normative studies there is a logical gulf fixed which no ingenuity can disguise and no juxtaposition in space or time bridge over. . . . But what, then is the significance of Economic Science? . . . [I]t provides, within its own structure of generalisations, no norms which are binding in practice. It is incapable of deciding as between the desirability of different ends. *It is fundamentally distinct from Ethics.* ([1935] 1948, 147–48, 151–52, italics added)

Here, in short, is the triumphant dissolution of an earlier ethical ideal. Robbins's claim is a reflection of that of John Neville Keynes who, in addressing explicitly "the relation between political economy and ethics," had insisted that "it is not, however, the function of the science to pass ethical judgments; and political economy, regarded as a positive science, may, therefore, be said to be independent of ethics" (1891, 60). Pigou had earlier taken much the same methodological position. He observed in his *Economics of Welfare* that "economic study . . . is a positive science of what is . . . not a normative science of what ought to be" ([1932] 1962, 5).

In Robbins's methodological position, and in the establishment of his unbridgeable distinction between facts and values, the pretense is perpetuated that the two are inviolably separable. But such a position raises an issue of significant methodological and philosophic import. No consideration arises, from that point of view, of the possibility that the thing that gives a fact its facticity is the value or the significance it has in the scheme of explanation of which it is a part. Brute facts constitute, from that point of view, basic epistemological data. But whether that is so remains very much open to philosophic discussion and to conceivable disagreement. The contrary proposition may well be sustained. Ontology may be prior to epistemology. Facticity may well be thought to depend on the realization and assignment of meaning. If that important issue is closed and declared to be off limits to the economist in the manner that Robbins proposed, then it may be judged that the intellectual discipline is impoverished before its exploration has got under way.

THREE CONTEMPORARY CRITIQUES AND ETHICAL IMPORT

Perspective on our present investigation will be enhanced by taking note of three different, or differently articulated, standpoints that characterize what is taken to be the scope and preoccupation of contemporary economics. The viewpoints raise a common, though in some respects a significantly differentiated, concern for methodological implications and their significance, and for the relevance to them of ethical presuppositions.

Letwin's "Intricate Mechanism"

First, the relationship between economics and questions of ethical foundations became, at a relatively early stage, substantially what William Letwin has described in his *The Origins of Scientific Economics*. "There can be no doubt," Letwin concludes,

that economic theory owes its present development to the fact that some men, in thinking of economic phenomena, forcefully suspended all judgments of theology, morality, and justice, [and] were willing to consider the economy as nothing more than an intricate mechanism, refraining for the while from asking whether the mechanism worked for good or evil. (1963, 147–48)

In Letwin's judgment, the threefold exclusion of what he refers to as "theology, morality, and justice" was not only prerequisite to the development of economic science, but it made of that science a clearly amoral discipline. The trilogy he invoked harks back to issues that we have already inspected. They have had an influential relevance for economic thought in its earlier formation. Justice and morality, whether or not they are taken to be theologically grounded as Letwin implied might once have been the case, warrant a reentry to economic argument. The grounds of justice remain, of course, for more extended consideration.

Admittedly, Letwin acknowledges, "it was exceedingly difficult to treat economics in a scientific fashion, since every economic act, being the action of a human being, is necessarily also a moral act" (1963, 148). But that was the task, as he saw it, that had to be accomplished in order that the subject as an academic and scientific discipline could develop. There had to be a separation of "positive from normative knowledge," a distinction drawn "between moral and technical knowledge" (1963, 147–48). In the course of effecting that separation and establishing that distinction, the economy came to be regarded substantially, as Letwin observes, as an intricate mechanism. The shadow of Walras the engineer-turned-economist was soon cast long across the discipline.

Of the widening breach, therefore, between economics and ethics there could be no doubt. The idiosyncratic expression of that breach in the attitude of Marshall, as that was explored in Keynes's evaluation of his position, has already been noted. Schumpeter has referred to "the process, as observed in the Cambridge milieu by which Christian belief, gently and without any acerbities, was dropped by the English intelligentsia" during Marshall's lifetime (1954, 772).

Hutchison's "Scientific Inquiry"

Second, Terence Hutchison has referred, in a not dissimilar but more explicitly methodological fashion, to the achievement of academic economics at Cambridge in the last quarter of the nineteenth century. He saw this as due to the fact that the great architects of the neoclassical theoretical system

conceived their task as belonging not in the realms of theology and metaphysics, but in clearing a site, and providing an agreed foundation for 'scientific' inquiry, and here . . . they drew no specially significant distinction between the two broad groups of sciences included under the very rough headings of the 'natural' and 'social' (or 'moral') sciences. (1953, 50)

Again in this evaluation the distinction is drawn between "theology and metaphysics" on the one hand and "scientific inquiry" on the other. This, of course, in what is essentially an invocation of scientism, is taking us to the heart of the epistemological problem in economics. It raises again the issue of the possibility of a value-free science of economics. It raises the question as to whether there exists an epistemological parity between the natural and the social sciences. Writing in 1938, Hutchison endeavored to hold economics securely to what he called "the Scientific Principle of Testability" ([1938] 1960, 143). In the 1960 reissue of his book he included a valuable survey of subsequent methodological debate, and in that he observed that "my views have become considerably less 'naturalist' . . . than they were . . . [but] the doctrines of a fundamental discontinuity in epistemological criteria between the study of nature and the study of man do not seem acceptable" ([1938] 1960, xi–xii. See also Hutchison 1977, 1984).

By way of partial summary at this point, the following can be said. Modern thought has worked out the bequest of the fact that the message of Smith in his *Moral Sentiments* on the one side was dislodged from its explicitly moral foundation by Ricardo's severe analytical a priorism and deductivism, if, indeed, Smith did not dislodge it himself in his subsequent *Wealth of Nations*. Sidgwick, Marshall, and others recanted from what Keynes brought into view as explicitly theological commitments, and Keynes forthrightly distanced himself from the need to articulate any ethical presuppositional basis. Now, and following with an almost severe necessity, Letwin's exclusion of "theology, morality, and justice," Hutchison's exclusion of "theology and metaphysics," and Robbins's unbridgeable gulf between ethics and economics have increasingly characterized the intellectual tone of the discipline.

Resnick and Wolff and Neo-Marxianism

Comparable issues are relevant in a third respect to the development of economics. The theism of earlier philosophy, tarnished though it was by Hume's well known skepticism and the aridity of eighteenth- and nineteenth-century deism, was roundly dislodged by Marx at the height of the midcentury socialist dissent. In the contemporary revival of Marxian economics a firm dissent is again registered from the possibility of an intrusion, in an absolutist and essentialist sense, of any religious-theological influences on economic thought. The ethical presuppositions that might be sustained by a religious motif require, therefore, careful delineation or qualification.

In the philosophic reconstruction of Marxism that Resnick and Wolff have proposed, a new conception of Marxian epistemology rejects what are there seen as all forms of essentialism or reductionism, establishing in their place what is referred to as an overdeterminationism (1985, 1987). That system of thought, informed as it is by explicitly postmodern motifs, understands all aspects of human existence, both as to ontology and epistemology, and, it appears, as to ethics, to be determined, or "overdetermined," by intersecting, interacting, and interintrusive influences from all other aspects. Indeed, the epistemological stance that Resnick and Wolff have carved implies that in some respects they have turned Marx on his head. For while Marx took over the Hegelian methodological dialecticism, he had replaced Hegel's idealistic dialectic by an explicitly formulated dialectical materialism. But among the innumerable forces and issues that, from the viewpoint that Resnick and Wolff have proposed, overdetermine all other aspects of being and knowing, the ideational and spiritual dimensions reenter as contributing elements. Hegel is thus in a sense reestablished. But what is meant in that scheme by the ideational and the spiritual distinguishes it from the religious presuppositions that earlier thought had embraced.

In their importation of related thought forms into economics, Resnick and Wolff have made a significant conceptual advance beyond the accepted stance of economic theorizing that, as Letwin and Hutchison have indicated, was earlier established. For Resnick and Wolff have clearly insisted that not only is it necessary to dissent from the claims for a value-free economics, but that, in the light of their epistemological perspective, a value-free economics is impossible. From the uniquely differentiated starting point from which their analysis emanates, therefore, their results converge with the conclusions that will be established in our ensuing argument. Economic theorizing, in short, cannot possibly be value-free.

Writing as economists with the intention of reconstructing economic thought, Resnick and Wolff characterize their achievement as follows:

> We have thus come full circle. Marx's famous warning in his *Contribution to the Critique of Hegel's Philosophy of Right* that the beginning of modern social criticism is the critique of religion is reaffirmed, only now in a new form. Marxist social criticism must begin with a critique of the deeply religious epistemological commitments and hence blindnesses inhibiting social analysis and hence social progress. Essentialist epistemology is perhaps a last stronghold of that religiosity that Marx knew had to be criticized to make way for the kind of radical social criticism which would be a condition for the existence of revolutionary social change. (1985, xxiv)

Marx's "famous warning" is here "reaffirmed in a new form." What are here referred to as the "deeply religious epistemological commitments" have reference, no doubt, to thought forms and motifs additional to what have traditionally been theologically connoted. But it is the religious commitment or presupposition in any form, in what the preceding reference implies is an absolutist or essentialist sense, that is the final "blindness inhibiting social analysis." In the philosophy of overdeterminationism, all aspects of human existence and awareness do contribute to their mutual realization. But, it is important to observe from that perspective, no one contributing motif is taken, or can be taken, to establish an absolute principle that can serve as a basis for the predication of meaning. Neo-Marxian thought in this dimension eschews, that is, all forms of reductionism. From such a standpoint, presumably, the Sidgwick-Marshallian recantation is to be applauded as opening the way to new possibilities of intellectual progress.

CONCLUDING EVALUATION

The immediate significance of the viewpoints we have inspected, as well as of other and related forms of post-Marxianism and various postmodernisms that have entered the discipline, has to do with their import for the issue with which we began. That concerns the extent to which, or the manner in which, economics can or should effectively address some suitably formulated ethical ideal. Or, as has been suggested, it concerns the extent to which an earlier commitment to an ethical ideal has been progressively dissolved. Overdeterminationism understands the economic individual to be, as is said, socially constituted, or, in other words, determined, as to his or her being and knowing and acting, by the very economic and socio-cultural processes of which he or she is a part. The point of that proposition is no doubt well taken, so far as it dissents from, for example, familiar Walrasian assumptions. Those are that individuals enter economic and market activities and relations as autonomous and exogenously-defined participants and are unaffected by the economic process in which they engage. But other issues remain.

The rigors of the passage of real time, and of the ignorance of the future in which economic decision making is bound, cast doubt on the severely staticized equilibrium theoretic systems to which economics is substantially committed. In that sense it is necessary to recast economic argument in the light of the reality that as time passes individuals do know different things in different ways, and that their economic participations are determined and affected as a result. But postmodernism, in many of its expressions, goes further. In the light of the fact that the individual is, as is said, socially constituted, it is frequently supposed that there does not exist a continuous human nature.

But while it may be granted that the economic individual is understood to be characterized by an epistemological discontinuity, meaning that he or she knows different things in different ways at different times, there remains, against that epistemological discontinuity, an ontological continuity. There remains, that is, what might be referred to as a continuity of mind. The importance of that conclusion rests in the fact that it takes us back to our primary concern. It is, in the last analysis, that ontological continuity that provides the grounding for ethics and responsibility. It is in that sense that caution is needed in interpreting the meaning, for example, of Georgescu-Roegen's claim that one of the aspects that "is likely to create insuperable analytical difficulties . . . in the model homo economicus . . . is that *man* is a continuously changing structure" (1966, 187).

The perspectives from which the ethico-economic relationship can be evaluated are partially established by the foregoing review of the positions that have been reached, and the manner in which they were reached, in the mainstream of the economics discipline. But that in itself provides only half of the initial perspective building that needs to be done. Additionally, it is necessary to inspect, at least in a summary fashion, the definitional and foundational concepts that are provided by the work of the moral philosophers. It is to that second aspect of the foundational structures that we turn immediately in the following chapter.

3 ETHICS AND ETHICAL JUDGMENTS

An evaluation of the relations that exist, or that potentially exist, between economics and ethics requires at least a summary review of the concepts, thought forms, and definitions of the ethicists and the moral philosophers. The objective of this chapter is to address that necessity and to provide a further aspect of the background for the more detailed discussions in the chapters in part III. The minimal philosophic vocabulary of this chapter, together with that of more technical economics in subsequent chapters, will provide a basis for communication between the respective disciplines.

THE CONTRIBUTION OF PHILOSOPHY TO ECONOMICS

In the somewhat more than half a century since Robbins ([1935] 1948), Harrod ([1938] 1950), and Hutchison ([1938] 1960) reawakened interest in economic methodology, a great deal of attention has been given to the intersection between economics and the philosophy of the natural sciences. Hutchison's recent and insightful *Changing Aims in Economics* (1992) sums up much of the debate. Between the earlier and the later dates Popper's hypothetico-deductive method, his method of conjectures and refutation and its dissent from an earlier positivism (1959), Kuhn's paradigm switches (1970), and Lakatos's methodology of scientific research programs (1970) have spawned extensive comment and evaluation (see Lakatos and Musgrave 1970; Latsis 1976; Blaug 1980; Boland 1982; Caldwell 1982, 1984; and the bibliographies cited). When Hausman prepared his recent anthology on *The Philosophy of Economics* it was presented as a "historical perspective on the methodology of economics" (1984, vii), and minimal, though very valuable, space was accorded issues of values and value judgments. To the extent that economic and philosophic scholarship have interacted, the bridge building has been done for the main part by those interested in questions of method and styles of analysis.

On the other hand, interest in the relation between economics and the philosophy of the moral sciences has been far less extensive. The prolific work of A.K. Sen has kept that interconnection alive (see Sen 1987), and issues of morality and justice have been explored (Rawls 1971; Nozick 1973, 1974; Rescher 1966; Etzioni 1986; Ball 1986). Hausman and McPherson have presented a valuable survey of recent literature and have raised a number of issues relating to "Economics and Contemporary Moral Philosophy" (1993). *The International Journal of Economics and Ethics* has contributed to the newly awakened interest in related areas. But to a very large extent economics as an analytical discipline has remained in the traditions that have argued for an essentially value-free enquiry. Robbins's rigorous separation of economics from ethics has substantially triumphed, though Sen, for example, has complained of the "impoverishment of economics related to its distancing from ethics" (1987, 57). He has observed in the same context that

moral acceptance of rights (especially rights that are valued and supported and not just respected in the form of constraints) may call for a systematic departure from self-interested behavior. Even a partial and limited move in that direction in actual conduct can shake the behavioural foundations of standard economic theory. (1987, 57)

Sen's arguments in that direction are now well known. His essay on "Rational Fools" ([1976–77] 1979) has alerted us to the wisdom of having regard not only to a narrowly conceived self-interest, but also to what he has referred to as sympathy and commitment in economic decisions and behavior.

At a minimum, the rightness or wrongness, or the propriety or otherwise, of economic behavior and policy depend quite clearly on the angle of vision with which relevant issues are addressed. It is not simply that, as has been frequently acknowledged, theoretical concepts are themselves value-laden. Nor is it simply that, as Weber put it, "the significance of cultural events [including, as he observed, economic events] presupposes a *value-orientation* towards those events. The concept of culture is a *value-concept*" (1984, 101). It is there that Weber's claims regarding "presuppositions" enter (1984, 102). The angle of vision undoubtedly plays its part in both the selection of areas of life experience worthy of scientific investigation and the interpretation of the meaning and significance of relevant data.

But on the level with which we are at present concerned, other and deeper issues are involved. They raise questions that the economics literature has to a large extent ignored. The need exists, when importing thought forms from the moral to the social sciences, to take into account the issues raised in the famous *Wertfreiheit* debates as to whether economics can or cannot be value-free. But beyond that, it is necessary to confront explicitly the formation of ethical criteria, the foundations from which they emanate, and the meaning and relevance of ethical concepts and constructs.

Why, in short, are ethical desiderata what they are? The importation of ethics to economics is not exhausted simply by a disagreement with Robbins's claim that the economist qua economist can pronounce only on the efficiency of means to achieve ends, and that he has no competence to adjudicate in relation to the ends themselves. The deeper issue has to do with the standpoint and the ethical criteria in terms of which the ends themselves are, or can be, evaluated. Pressing for attention is the question of what is to be understood by the very concept of the ethical. It is necessary to address the processes by which the criteria of the good or the bad, the right or the wrong, the acceptable standards of moral approval, disapproval, duty, or obligation, can be established.

DEVELOPMENTS IN ETHICAL THEORY

The relative weakness of the association between economics and ethics is no doubt due in part to the historical uncertainty of the moral sciences as to where they stood, or should stand, and what bequest they might make to other disciplines. Gewirth has done much in recent times to stabilize and reorganize that field of study ([1972] 1976, 1978, 1982, 1984), and the summing-up comment by Regis in his edited volume on *Gewirth's Ethical Rationalism* points to some of the more significant aspects of the contemporary situation.

Of the several different features that distinguish twentieth-century moral philosophy from that of previous decades, probably none is more important and portentous than its skepticism about whether any moral principles at all can be known or proved to be true. This skepticism has taken many forms: emotivism and other noncognitivisms, intuitionism, subjectivism, prescriptionism, and the recent practice of laying down ultimate moral principles by fiat or mere say-so. . . . Until very lately, moral theory was characterized by a disinterest in systematization . . . [but] Gewirth . . . principally in his book *Reason and Morality* has advanced an ethical system in the classic sense: a body of hierarchically structured descriptive and prescriptive claims . . . the purpose of the system is to derive normative ethical propositions that are rationally warranted. (1984, 1)

Clearly, the literature of moral philosophy and those areas of study that bear on the status of ethical concepts has been influenced by recent developments in the philosophic disciplines. These have replaced an earlier interest in classic forms of system-building by a concern with the analysis of language and meaning. The preoccupation of philosophers with the meaning of terms has given rise to what is referred to as meta-ethics, or the study of the categories that attach ethical meaning and significance to things or outcomes, or to actions and behavior. Gewirth has provided an analysis of what is involved, and the following comments on that level are indebted to Gewirth's summaries.

The meta-ethical concern with the status of concepts is to be distinguished from the application of those concepts to the formation of ethically acceptable rules of conduct or policy. On the former level, the meta-ethical statements may derive from varying philosophic commitments or persuasions. Intuitionists, for example, claim that an individual possesses a direct grasp of moral qualities. The moral rightness or wrongness of actions is in that case intuited directly, without any intervention of a consideration of the value or rightness of consequences. To engage different terminology and a somewhat different though related dichotomy, distinctions have been drawn between cognitivism on the one hand and noncognitivism on the other. The former affirms that ethical statements constitute a form of knowledge, in the sense that they can be shown to be true or false. Noncognitivism, on the contrary, understands that ethical statements simply express attitudes or commands. In the terms we have just introduced, intuitionism may be taken as a form of cognitive meta-ethical theory. Certain things, in that case ethical criteria, are known intuitively.

As to normative ethics, distinctions are to be drawn between deontological theories on the one hand and teleological theories on the other. That dichotomy, it was seen at an earlier stage, establishes an important distinction between ways of looking at things in an economic context. The meaning of the terms therefore provides an important starting point in the interconnection of ethics and economics. Teleological theories, the description of which derives from the Greek word that is transliterated "teleios" and means "end" or "purpose," stress the goal or the objective that is in view in decision and action. In the economics literature, utilitarianism, for example, is essentially a teleological theory or doctrine. The meaning of the term explains why teleological theories have been referred to as consequentialist theories in economic ethics.

Deontological theories, on the other hand, stress not the objective in view in human behavior, but the obligation or duty involved in actions that are taken. The description in this case derives from the Greek word that is transliterated "deontos," meaning "obligatory." Deontological theories, therefore, hold as basic concepts the notions of oughtness, while teleological theories focus attention on what is valuable or worthy in itself, or can be seen as conducing to desired ends. In the latter case, moral judgment is understood to be justified by its relation to the goodness of the consequences that are capable of being achieved by the actions in view. The focus on the consequences of actions means that utilitarianism is, in many of its expressions, a consequentialist economic doctrine.

In addition to the distinction between deontological and teleological theories, attention is frequently given to the axiological aspects or content of ethical claims. Axiology refers to what is good or of value. It thus generates ethical claims that focus on the inherent goodness of outcomes, such, for example, as happiness or pleasure or, in some sense, satisfaction. Forms of hedonistic ethics or hedonism, sometimes associated philosophically with eudaemonism, or the ethics of personal well-being or happiness, accordingly come into view at that point.

But from whatever viewpoint or philosophic orientation such issues are addressed, whether informed by deontology, teleology, or axiology, the question that comes to the fore is that of the nature of moral judgments that are derived from them. Judgments of goodness or rightness, that is, might be understood to proceed from any of a number of grounds. But for purposes of the impact of ethics and economics it is important to distinguish also between two other related questions: first, judgments as to what is good or right on moral or ethical grounds; and second, judgments on other grounds that might be thought to be relevant to specific situations. Such other grounds may be those of legality or prudence or religious persuasion. Elster has spoken of the distinctions between "moral norms," "social norms," and "legal norms." In Elster's construction, social norms, which must be shared by other people in order to warrant approval or disapproval, differ from "private norms" or private rules or behavior habits (1989, 100). It is quite possible, of course, that what might be held in view as moral grounds may be inseparable from, in the sense that they are themselves determined by, religious persuasion. That may be the case in certain forms of transcendental ethics.

For our present studies, what we are now contemplating as the ground of uniquely moral judgments, as distinct from legal or prudential judgments, will be brought into view. What is legal or prudential from certain points of view might not necessarily be judged to be morally right or acceptable. Certain forms or structures of income distribution, for example, may satisfy legal and institutional criteria and standards, while serious questions may arise as to the level of morality inherent in them. Or to take another example, certain forms of employment procedures and practices, while they satisfy criteria of legality and institutional arrangements, may nevertheless, by virtue of implicit forms of discrimination contained within them, offend acceptable ethical desiderata.

On a further and an economically relevant level, the literature that has addressed the nature of moral judgments has raised a much debated question by asking whether such judgments are, or should be, universalizable. It is possible to conceive of formal conditions, it has been argued, that render the judgments universalizable, or relevant and ethically operative in society and applicable to social conduct in general. The categorical imperative of Kant that was referred to in the preceding chapter was viewed in this way as universalizable. To the extent that universalizability is claimed, the relevant ethical mandates have become essentially deontological in the sense in which that term has been defined. They establish in themselves, that is to say, conditions and mandates of obligatory behavior.

It is possible, however, to look at the formation of moral rules and judgments from a quite different point of view. The preceding discussion has had in view what might be referred to as formal characteristics or conditions in ethical theory. Emphasis might be placed, on the other hand, on what have been termed material conditions. In that case, some characteristic of material goodness that might be realized by the institution of certain rules of behavior is contemplated. From that position, rules involved could be taken to reflect what are primarily axiological or teleological considerations. They could at the same time be taken to bear primarily on the interests of the persons taking the actions contemplated, or on the interests of society at large.

Of course the notion of what is good or right, or what should be sought after in the formulation of moral rules, may again stand in various possible relations to more basic philosophic positions. Such notions may be influenced, for example, by such conceptions as Plato's well-known Idea of the Good, which he promulgated as part of his philosophy of ideal forms. Or as theologians have historically observed, goodness might be located in the idea of God, as with Augustine, or in conceptions of natural law, as with Aquinas. The latter consistently relied more on the somewhat down to earth philosophy of Aristotle than on the idealism of Plato. With Aristotle, he understood the goodness of a thing to consist in its conformation to the end it was capable of achieving, or in the intrinsic nature and quality of its potential and full development.

In the philosophy of Kant a quite different basis of ethical formulation existed. While he had not eliminated reference to God from his work, God was for him logically dispensable. That point was made in the preceding chapter by adducing what was referred to as Kant's conception, on the level of epistemology, of the autonomy of the individual. But to bring together some of these different possible bases of ethical rules, Kant with Plato, it can be said, took the position that God approves of actions because they are morally right, not that they are morally right because God approves of them. The point of difference can be made in that way as an instance of the distinction between what can be called a Kantian immanentistic or rationalistic ethic on the one hand and a transcendental ethic on the other.

The question also arises as to the manner in which right and proper action, or the satisfaction of acceptable ethical standards, might be thought to depend on criteria established by social and cultural development. It could be understood, for example, that such historical movements as the Renaissance, the Reformation, or the industrial revolution gave rise to the acceptance of ethical standards, of either deontological or teleological kinds, determined by various historical forces.

Such historically or culturally determined standards may characterize forms of egalitarianism, elitism, socialism, individualism, and egoistic or universalistic utilitarianism. By the latter is meant an expression of utilitarianism that addresses the good of the larger society. In egoistic utilitarianism, on the other hand, the good of the individual is principally in view. By way of further example, Marxism holds that moral criteria, along with economic criteria, are determined by underlying ideological thought structures in a uniquely dialectical sense. Marxism sees a dialectical interaction of the relations of production, or the dominant economic and social class structure and property relations on the one hand, with the forces of production, or technological and economic production processes, on the other. Or with Freud, turning aside from the Marxian materialism, moral data might be seen as emanating from parental and social conditioning.

In view of our reference in the preceding chapter to Keynes's embrace of the ethico-philosophic position of Moore, it might be noted that Moore advanced what, in the terms we have just explored, can be referred to as a form of axiological intuitionism. It was a form of cognitive theory, that is, that understood goodness as an indefinable property that was grasped by direct intuition. As to the normative implications that followed, Moore focused on the notion of what was instrumentally good, implying that what one ought to do was to act in such a way as to achieve a maximum of intrinsic goodness. In taking this position Moore is in effect a utilitarian, in that he sees one's duty as that of bringing about as much good as possible.

Other forms of intuitionism, such as Prichard's deontological intuitionism that Gewirth has explored at more length, argue that one's intuition is an apprehension of what one ought to do in order to satisfy intuitively perceived obligation. Such positions, however, might be considered defective in that they do not advance any ultimate or recognizable reason for one's moral duty or obligation. To the extent that a position such as that taken by Prichard grounds morality in a sense of obligation that is immediate or underived, or that refuses to have any regard to consequences of action, it is clearly distanced from the utilitarian or teleological emphases that have been common to the economics discipline.

A difficulty confronting ethical theories of the intuitive kind is their failure to provide any means of taking account of conflicting intuitions. An alternative development in ethical theory has given rise to a so-called ethical naturalism. In that perspective, the notion is encountered that moral judgments are empirical statements and that moral knowledge can be brought very close to, if not made a part of, natural science. By that it is meant that moral attributes can be identified with empirical qualities. Such a procedure is instanced in the system of Aristotle, who understood goodness to be something objective that inhered in a thing's realizing its true end or full development. It was that kind of basic Aristotelian position that Aquinas took over and emphasized. But what is important at this point is that such forms of supposedly objective material goodness, such as, to take a modern example, that food is good and that the provision of food is good because of the purpose it serves, also suffer from rather obvious defects.

Such materialistic theories tend clearly to emphasize goodness as referable primarily to individual positions and actions and to individual benefits. They may fail, as a result, to take adequate account of situations in which social interrelations and larger dimensions of benefit are at issue. Moreover, it may well be the case that goodness, understood in materialistic terms to inhere in the capacity of a thing to realize its full development and thereby contribute to individual satisfaction, may inhere in things that are morally reprehensible and, on purportedly adequate grounds, deserve to be condemned. The pragmatism of the American philosopher James and the naturalism of Dewey, for example, fall under such a critique. They see goodness essentially in the ability of a thing to satisfy demand or to inhere in any object of interest, quite apart from normative aspects of value. As a result, they can too easily offend against criteria of moral acceptability.

With arguments such as these in view a relevant economic question can be explored. It can be asked on such a level whether all of the uninhibited forces of market supply and demand are beyond moral evaluation, approval, or condemnation. Buchanan, for example, has recently drawn a distinction between market efficiency and market morality. It is possible to "make the case for the market solely on the grounds that it allocates resources and distributes products most efficiently, eschewing any attempt to establish its moral superiority." But it is at the same time possible and consistent to argue that "it ought to be reformed or even abandoned, even if doing so would result in a loss of efficiency" (1985, 3). It might be agreed, for example, that exploitation of addictive drug traffic or other forms of vice should attract moral condemnation, even though they may, in themselves, provide forms of satisfaction and meet market criteria of supply and demand. In short, there may well be grounds for objection, in the context of market analysis, to Dewey's position that nothing is intrinsically good or bad, and that moral standards are like rules of grammar that are capable of change with changing customs and conditions (see Clark 1992, 82).

Our discussion to this point has focused in several ways on what were referred to as cognitive ethical theories. They raise in one way or another the possibility that moral judgments can be understood not only to be forms of knowledge, but to be assessable as to their truth or falsity. If, however, one were to reject the notions of cognitive ethical theories in that sense, or the claims that moral terms have descriptive meaning, an alternative and very different stance might be taken. It might be decided, that is, that no conclusive justification for moral judgments exists. In that case, statements that purport to have a moral import would be understood simply as expressing feelings or emotions or attitudes. They would not, then, be open to any kind or degree of verification, and they would not be cognitively meaningful. Moral statements would in such a scheme of things be regarded simply as commending or commanding statements.

In the view of the noncognitivists, therefore, the primary meaning of the good is that it is not descriptive, but, on the contrary, simply evaluative or prescriptive. In that respect, such theories have been thought by some ethicists to overcome the problem of cognitive theories, in that the latter provide no means of overcoming moral disagreements. But it remains to be considered also, of course, what constitutes or provides the grounds or bases on which noncognitivist commands or commendations do themselves have ultimate and sustainable meaning or validity.

ECONOMICS AND NORMATIVE ETHICAL CRITERIA

The meta-ethical concepts and categories advanced in the preceding discussion are reflected in normative ethical positions. The basic question on the normative level has to do with criteria for deciding whether actions, or, in our present context, economic decisions and policies, are morally right or wrong. Or equivalently, we are concerned now with the moral content of actual economic decisions, actions, and choices and with the grounds of relevant evaluative judgments. In the context of economic argument the question arises, not only whether economic actions are in themselves morally good or bad, but whether economic society should be organized in one way or another in order that institutional actions and policies are justifiable from a moral point of view.

The reference in that question is not simply or solely to possible forms of economic organization, such as market capitalism, systems of economic collectivism, or mixed economies. It is observable that in recent times and in various parts of the world movements from collectivism to forms of market capitalism have occurred. Or it might be said that in the former Soviet Union, for example, a movement has occurred from state capitalism to private capitalism. What needs to be considered at this point are the ways in which, within whatever form of organization exists, both private and public policies and outcomes meet ethical criteria that might, for one reason or another, be held.

This points to a number of implied questions. First, it may be asked what, among the list of the things the economic system is capable of producing, it is or is not morally or ethically proper or desirable to produce. It may be asked, in other words, whether some things are or are not to be understood as good in themselves. Or secondly, it may be debated among economists whether such a question can be legitimately raised at all. That touches, of course, on the issue of ends versus means, and on whether again the economist qua economist can legitimately have anything to say about the ends. But it raises also the recognizably difficult question of whether ethical considerations can or should have anything to say about the relative ranking of desired or achievable ends. To put that highly sensitive issue in different terms, questions of the possible rankings of desirability of actions and policies may appear to attach different degrees of morality to different economic judgments and decisions. Ethical decisions on levels such as these are capable of bringing into focus differences between objective and subjective, or between absolute and relative, ethical evaluative approaches.

To suppose that certain things are desirable in themselves, or that hierarchies of rankings exist among desirable things, is to take what we noted in the preceding section as an axiological view of ethics. An example may be found in the different possible outputs that the nation's economic resources may be used to produce. Such a question is directly concerned with values and the relative values of things. It is, in an important sense, the kind of attitude that is basic to what we have seen is a teleological view of ethics. In different expressions, such a viewpoint might emphasize as the grounding for judgments of rightness or wrongness such axiological objectives, on a microeconomic level, as pleasure, happiness, power, or prestige. In relation to economic society as a whole, those objectives may relate to different levels or distributions of economic benefit and welfare.

In the light of the concepts that were raised in the preceding section, the normative criteria that now come under review may be understood to be deontological on the one hand or teleological on the other. The criteria of rightness or obligation that deontological theories establish may raise difficulties, however, by virtue of an implicit ethical pluralism. Difficulty may arise in taking account of moral disagreements, or in resolving tensions between conflicting obligations. It might be supposed at that point that such tensions can be resolved by adopting a monistic deontological ethic, where a single non-formal criterion of rightness is proposed. Such a monistic criterion might be, for example, human dignity. Or other deontological conceptions, such as address the questions of equity or equality, may be proposed. In the contemporary cultural climate of individualism and liberal democracy, the principle of consent may be elevated to criterion status. Action may be thought to be obligatory, that is, where the individual who has the obligation to perform a certain action has consented to do so. The keeping of promise, or adherence to the terms of economic contracts, are cases in point.

But monistic theories of the kind we have just referred to, while they appear to avoid difficulties inherent in the pluralistic theories by providing a way of resolving tensions between conflicting obligations, do themselves encounter difficulties. They raise the residual problem of explaining why the monistic principle they enunciate should be regarded as providing the ultimate grounding of obligation.

The difficulties that occur on these levels might be thought to be relieved by a more formalized deontological theory. By that it is meant that the appeal of the theory is to the logically necessary, or, that is, the formal relations between what might be held as acceptable or proper moral judgments. The principle of consistency might in that case be invoked, and the claim made that actions are not rationally justifiable, and that a duty to perform them does not therefore exist, where the performance would involve a contradiction. But that, of course, may do no more than shift to a different level the problem of conflict of obligations. An important attempt to address and to implement such a criterion has occurred in the history of ethical theory in terms of what has already been referred to as the principle of universalizability. The categorical imperative of Kant that was noted at an earlier point is an influential instance of the argument.

The problem with such a categorical imperative, however, is that it may be understood to apply rigorously to all similar individuals in similar positions or circumstances. But that in turn raises the difficulty of reaching agreement in every case on whether and when the necessary full conditions of similarity exist. The obligatory ethic could easily be vacated by claims that differences of circumstances or of individual conditions and characteristics exist. A high degree of arbitrariness may thus enter the ethical argument that it was thought the deontological insistence would resolve. The hopefully efficient principle of universalizability, that is, does not of itself explain what similarities are to be counted as relevant and determinative in differing situations.

In certain economic situations, however, the principle of universalizability may make a significant contribution to resolving ethical dilemmas. In the matter of income and wealth distribution, for example, or in what has been referred to in the economic and ethical literature as distributive justice, the principle may have significant application. This application leaves open, of course, the question of the underlying ground or principle of obligation, or the ground that is understood to be universalizable as the relevant determinative or deontic principle. That deeper principle or criterion may be, as previously suggested, a notion of equity or human dignity or fairness.

It follows, in such a case as that of distributive justice, that the ethic of universalizability cannot be what we have referred to as monistic. It cannot establish in itself, that is to say, a reliable guide to action. It is necessary to articulate and to hold along with it some subsidiary substantive principle, perhaps of the kind we have suggested. Or such a subsidiary or substantive principle might have reference to merit, social class, elitism, need, or other

cultural criteria that might have been determined by historical development or precedent.

In this connection, however, a possible residual problem remains.
Consistency may be logically satisfied in the universalization of what, on
grounds that are purportedly adequate, may be judged to be morally
wrong. Would it be morally acceptable, for example, to universalize as an
ethical criterion the principle of not telling the truth or not keeping a
promise? To do so, of course, would fly in the face of every tradition of
trust on which economic transactions and relations have been based. Or
what would be the implications of such a criterion for, say, economic contracts or the annual payment of income tax?

SOME ECONOMIC EXAMPLES

Economics, to the extent that it has been ethically self-conscious, has vac-
illated between what we have explored as deontological criteria and conditions and those established by teleological or consequentialist theories.
Frequently, as in forms of utilitarianism, the teleological theory focuses on
an aggregative principle, such as the greatest good for society as a whole.
An example from economics is the argument that those actions or policies
that result in an increase in the level of gross domestic product are automatically, and for that reason, desirable. Questions of the distribution of
economic benefits within society may to that extent be set aside. Or they
may be submerged by notions of compensation principles to which the sub-
discipline of welfare economics has frequently referred. Or in other
expressions, the consequentialist principle may envisage the greatest good
for the greatest number of members of society. In one way or another a
maximizing principle, such as is frequently espoused in the logic of economic analysis, is generally present.

But at the same time as teleology has exerted a heavy influence on the
development of economic thought and policy, the fact that the question of
value has had extensive currency in economics has introduced markedly
axiological emphases. Hedonistic criteria of pleasure, for example, associated perhaps with objectives of self-interest or even selfishness, might be
thought to be morally acceptable. But such an axiological criterion might
easily offend against alternative notions of what the good entails. Such ethical criteria may well be a long way from what we observed as Adam
Smith's notion of sympathy or fellow feeling as the cementing elements of
society. Such criteria may ignore completely what we have referred to as
human and economic solidarity.

It is at that point that economic theory has struggled to clarify, or has
been content at times to confuse, what have been referred to as egoistic
and universalistic utilitarianism. But it has been clarified, by Sen among

Europe in the late nineteenth century. That episode in economic contro- versy is important for its anticipation of the more modern insistence on the need to maintain a distinction between normative and positive economics. During the earlier decades of the nineteenth century the German histori- cal school (Wilhelm Roscher, 1817–94; Bruno Hildebrand, 1812–78; Karl Knies, 1821–98) had dissented in broad terms from the severely deductive a priorism of the English classical economics, as that had come to maturity in Ricardo ([1817] 1911) and his contemporaries. The historical school pro- gram was concerned with the investigation of national histories and the derivation of relevant historical laws. In that endeavor the interdepen- dence of legal, political, cultural, and economic influences was deemed to be important. It was not possible, that is, to develop a system of economic explanation that was applicable to all time and all places and all situations. In the historical school's conception of things, relativism in economic explanation was thus paramountly important. The conception of discover- able economic laws, moreover, was value-impregnated in the sense we have just observed.

That earlier historical school was succeeded by a younger generation that included Gustav Schmoller (1838–1917) and Carl Menger (1840–1921), whose *Grundsätze* ([1871] 1950) was one of the foundation pillars of the marginalist school that emerged in the 1870s. Menger's *Studies in the Methods of the Social Sciences and of Political Economy in Particular* appeared in 1883 (the year of the death of Marx and the birth of John Maynard Keynes). In that work Menger withdrew the endorse- ment he had given in his earlier *Grundsätze* to the German historical school and to Roscher in particular (see Rothschild 1993, 22; Hutchison 1953, 145ff.; Spiegel 1991, 530). Menger attempted to insist on a firm sep- aration between historical and statistical economics on the one hand and theoretical economics on the other. In a sense, therefore, Menger's empirical and deductive methods are to be set against, for example, Schmoller's historical economics. It was this methodological clash between Menger and Schmoller that laid the basis for what became referred to as the *Methodenstreit*, or methodological controversy, of the late nineteenth century.

Arising from those debates was the *Wertfreiheit* principle, that of the separation of economic argument and questions of empirical economic knowledge from what were taken to be nonscientific questions or matters of value judgment and value elements. Purely economic statements were to be rigorously separated from value statements. An important contribu- tion and a very strong insistence on the separation of scientific-economic from value statements appeared in the work of Max Weber (1864–1920) whose " 'Objectivity' in Social Science and Social Policy" (see Weber 1949; excerpted in Hausman 1984, 99–112, q.v. for the following statements) has exerted continuing influence.

Weber begins with the familiar distinction between ends and means and goes on to observe that in social science "we are interested in an *empirical science of concrete reality*" (1984, 100). It is true that "the significance of cultural events presupposes a *value-orientation* towards those events" (101), and Weber speaks of "the *value-ideas* in the light of which we view 'culture' [and of] the logically necessary rootedness of all historical entities in 'evaluative ideas'" (103). He holds to "the transcendental presupposition of every *cultural science* [that] lies . . . in the fact that we are *cultural beings*." And "all knowledge of cultural reality . . . is always knowledge from *particular points of view*" (104).

But a large part of Weber's plea for "objectivity" in economics as a social science rests in his complaint against "the naive self-deception of the specialist who is unaware that [his standpoint] is due to the evaluative ideas with which he unconsciously approaches his subject matter" (104). Weber cautions against "the naturalistic prejudice that every concept in the cultural sciences should be similar to those in the exact natural sciences" (109), and he observes on "the fantastic claim . . . occasionally made for economic theories" (109) in that regard. He does, however, insist on a correspondence of method in an important sense. This is that the social sciences, to the extent that they present scientific propositions (that he discusses extensively under the rubric of "ideal types" (111, see Spiegel 1991, 430–31)) should be kept scrupulously free of value judgments, or judgments of personal preferences and political valuations.

Weber is thus to be seen as a strong advocate of the *Wertfreiheit* principle of the separation of scientific economics and value judgments. We have observed in the foregoing his recognition that personal "evaluative ideas" influence the standpoint that economists take in their scientific work, and we have noted the cautions that he raises in relation to them. But the question arises as to what are the nature and sources of such possibly tarnishing value positions, and what might be the extent to which they are or are not unavoidable and perhaps legitimate. It may be quite impossible, in other words, to adhere rigorously to the *Wertfreiheit* principle in practice. To put the issue on a different but closely related level, it may be difficult or even impossible to hold consistently to the necessary separation, as it has been widely claimed, between the normative and the positive in economic argument. Weber's principle of value-free economic theorizing may itself be recognizable only as an ideal form. Alternatively, it might be concluded that the attempt to distinguish rigidly between the normative and the positive should be surrendered as a principle of methodological procedure.

The discussion in the economics literature that has ensued on all these matters, from the value-free perspectives that were thus introduced, has not separated out clearly an important and necessary distinction. That is the distinction between what have been referred to as value judgments in general and ethical judgments in particular. The more general formulations have to do with judgments of legality, political persuasion, ideological commitment, personal preferences, and psychological predilections. Discussions of "norms" have appeared, and a separation of "social norms" from "moral norms" has been noted (Elster 1989, 100). In their recent review article on "Taking Ethics Seriously: Economics and Contemporary Moral Philosophy" (1993), Hausman and McPherson have emphasized the relation between morality and economic assumptions or principles of rationality, and they have discussed the moral significance of economic theorizing on such levels as individual preferences, utility, equality, competitive analysis, and justice. That highly valuable and analytically sophisticated review article begins a probe to the foundation questions of why moral actions and ethically supportable principles are what they are. It points to the possible reasons why ethically sustainable claims may be entered against, or in support of, economic behavior and policy. But the economics literature has for the main part nodded at ethical questions and desiderata from a more remote distance. Case studies of ethico-economic applications on these levels have been discussed insightfully in Dworkin, Bermant, and Brown (1977).

The source and character of value judgments and, as he refers to it, bias in economic argument, have been surveyed in an ordered fashion by Hutchison (1964, 51–119). Without committing him to all of the argument that follows, a number of relevant issues may be observed at this stage. First, Hutchison, in the interests of preserving to every extent possible the normative-positive distinction, was very much concerned to wring from economic argument the kinds of value judgments and ethical statements that "cannot be tested or refuted inter-subjectively in the same way as the 'positive' statements of science." He followed "Popper's 'demarcation criterion'" to mark off " 'scientific' statements from 'non-scientific' statements and proposals (including ethical statements and value-judgments)" (1964, 52).

Joan Robinson and numerous other economists had claimed the same dependence on Popper's demarcation criterion (Robinson, 1962, 3). Admittedly, "this is certainly not to say that ethical statements or value-judgments are 'nonsensical,' or undiscussable, or beyond any rational examination," and a candid examination of them was desirable at the point and on the level of recommended economic policy. But it was necessary, as Hutchison saw it, to "demarcate or separate out for discussion the positive from the normative-evaluative elements" (1964, 53). The sanitization of the normative-positive distinction is here presented in particularly clear fashion.

Second, value judgments or forms of prescientific presuppositions undoubtedly enter into the economist's selection of areas of study deemed worthy of "scientific" investigation. Judgments enter also, though their ethical content may be less clearly distinguishable, in the decision as to methods of research procedure and the presentation of results. Ethical propriety no doubt enters in relation to the scrupulosity with which the research activity and procedure are allowed to provide the answer, rather than allowing an initially posited answer to determine an improperly selected or biased presentation of data or results. Of course, it is well understood that various questions, some quite different from those initially proposed, may arise in and during, and may be properly provoked by, the progress of research. But while questions inevitably arise in such a way in well-conducted research, the answers to them, if the distinctions we have raised are to be preserved, should not be impregnated with illegitimate value judgments and biases.

It follows also, as Myrdal, for example, has clarified in his *The Political Element in the Development of Economic Theory* ([1953] 1971), that influences from ideologies or prescientific vision enter into economic argument and theorizing. Relevant at that stage is the much discussed question of the extent to which the nineteenth-century economics, together with its reflection in contemporary theorizing, is to be seen as an apologia for capitalism and its class interest. But ideological commitments and prescientific persuasions are clearly capable of projecting into scholarly activity a heavy infusion of moral value judgments. They cause an interweaving of the normative and the positive in what might otherwise be conceived to be unarguably positive statements. Ricardo and his automatic harmonies as they were influenced by ubiquitous Say's Law assumptions, Marx in his uniquely idiosyncratic analytic formulations, Keynes in his concern for underemployment, and Hayek and the neo-Austrians in their economics of the market, along with their notion of plan coordination and market equilibrium, all saw things from differently describable points of view.

Widely different visions of the economic world, informed by different conceptions of legitimate starting points and value judgments, clearly lie behind different theoretical formations. The same issues are highly relevant to the debate that has ensued regarding the importability to economics of the methodologies of the natural sciences. It was observed at an earlier point that the most extensive exchange between philosophers and economists has taken place on the level of the philosophy of science. It is the question of methods and styles of analysis that has absorbed economists' interest, and not the questions of ethics and moral philosophy (see Boland 1982; Friedman 1953; Hausman 1984; Hutchison [1938] 1960, 1984, 1992; Lakatos and Musgrave 1970; Lakatos 1970).

Myrdal, as has been noted, made the claim that in economics and the social sciences "our very concepts are value-loaded" (1958, 1, quoted in Hutchison 1964, 69). His argument takes up the important question of the relation between facts, facticity, and value.

Valuations enter into social analysis, not only when conclusions concerning policy are drawn, but already in the theoretical endeavour to establish what is objectively true—in the choice of a field of enquiry, the selection of assumptions, *even the decision as to what is a fact and what is a value.* (1961, 274, quoted in Hutchison 1964, 69, italics added)

Myrdal here recognizes that economists approach their problems of theory-building and research with political and ethical presuppositions. The question that confronts the economist, as it does also the interpreter and user of his results, is whether those initial presuppositions can be effectively separated from the scientific content of the economist's work. It is the question whether value-free concepts reside in the analytical economist's tool kit (to adapt a phrase from Joan Robinson [1933] 1969, 1), and whether a "disciplined subject, free, or as practicably free as possible, of value-loads" (Hutchison 1964, 70) can be achieved.

But not only do political, philosophic, and ethical presuppositions in large degree determine the economist's stance as he approaches his subject and therefore his research agenda and results. A high degree of presuppositional influence is undoubtedly present at the very foundations of economic argument in other respects. For example, a precommitment to forms of economic individualism, or to collectivist planning, liberal market capitalism or libertarianism, the inevitability of aggregative economic disharmony, or notions of degrees of equity or equality and justice, all have potential and deeply determinative influence.

On more technical levels also, such pretheoretic commitments may predispose an economist to or against a variety of initial positions. These may be, for example, a demand-pull or a cost-push explanation of inflation, the imagined effectiveness of monetary or fiscal policy, or forms and degrees of market competitiveness and antitrust regulation. On another level, such precommitments may dispose the economist to focus his or her attention, for purposes of achieving high degrees of economic explanation, on the long run or the short (see Vickers, 1991, 1994). An economist may be Malthusian in holding to the analytical priority of the immediate or the short run, or Ricardian in his or her preoccupation with the long run outcomes of economic relations. Or a Marshallian perspective may be adopted in an attempt to mediate between the analytical pressures and influences of such different possible runs.

The practicing applied economist, of course, most usually imagines himself to be quite uninfluenced by such pretheoretical commitments. He works as a technician with a technical analytical apparatus. Lagrangian constrained extremum analysis is taken, for example, to be a quite value-free procedure. But the economist, by importing predeterminative value judgments into his or her work, will be influenced in general by idiosyncratic conceptions of desirable social aims, to the achievement of which economics as a discipline might be thought capable of making some contribution. To the extent that such aims are determinative, even though they might not be precisely articulated at every turn, the economist's work that is imagined to be technical and value-free takes on, to use previous thought forms, a decided teleological and axiological character. Certain kinds of work, and certain kinds of objectives that are held in view in that work, then become determinative by reason of the qualitative character of the outcomes to which it is hoped or thought they might lead. The implicit judgment regarding the value content of the ends in view gives what we earlier termed a consequentialist flavor to the investigative enterprise.

It is commonplace in economic discussion to set off such conceptions of achievable ends against the means that might be employed to achieve them. It is frequently supposed that while ethical or other value judgments may influence the conceptions of the ends, the means may generally be held to be value-free. The ends may be value-impregnated, but a value-neutrality attaches to the means. But Myrdal again has made the contrary point that

it is simply not true that only ends are the object of valuations and that means are valued only as instrumental to ends. In any human valuation means have, in addition to their instrumental value, independent values as well. The value-premiss which has to be introduced in order to allow policy conclusions to be reached from factual analysis has therefore to be a valuation of means as well as ends. (1958, 210–11, quoted in Hutchison 1964, 109)

A position such as Myrdal has taken has two implications. First, concealed value judgments may reside in the means, such, for example, as a preference for monetary over fiscal policy as a contracyclical policy instrument; and second, value judgments or premises may determine the economic institutional framework through which the economy, and therefore policies to affect the economy, function. Moreover, the nonneutrality of the means turns also on the reality that the use of different kinds of means will itself have different kinds of longer run effects on the structure and functioning of the economic system. It is hardly possible to be Machiavellian in economics and treat the means as amoral, assuming as a result that they are justified by the ends. In that respect Hutchison has quoted Huxley to good effect:

The end cannot justify the means, for the simple and obvious reason that the means employed determine the nature of the ends produced. . . . The means whereby we try to achieve something are at least as important as the end we wish to attain. Indeed they are even more important. For the means employed inevitably determine the nature of the result achieved. ([1938] 1965, 9, 52, quoted in Hutchison 1964, 110)

Moreover, it is clear on even a casual reflection that what are conceived to be ends in relation to a given argument or enquiry may serve as means on another level. From certain points of view, and against relevant pretheoretical commitments, a collectivist economic arrangement on the one hand, or a freely functioning market system on the other, may be taken as ends in view when certain policy attitudes or schemes of regulation are proposed. Those different possible ends, in turn, may be understood as means to the realization of more ultimate ends of justice or fairness in the distribution of income or wealth. It is hardly possible in such a situation to speak of the value-loaded character of ends, but the value-neutrality of means. Any number of other means versus ends relationships may be imagined.

SOME ECONOMIC EXAMPLES

It follows from the discussion of the preceding section that value judgments, including ethical judgments as well as judgments as to social norms that might be differently defined, are inevitably present in economic argument. Differences of view exist regarding the extent to which all such judgments can be, or should be, separated out in the course of economic analysis. An important application of the question exists in the widespread employment of utility theory or theories of preference orderings. These may be employed to explain, if not to justify, the working of the market system, or they may be adapted to more ambitious tasks such as that of inventing theories of aggregative economic welfare. At that latter stage, economic utility may or may not be reckoned to serve as an effective proxy for more comprehensive measures of welfare or well-being. These theories may lead at the same time to notions of interpersonal comparisons of utility and welfare, and to supposedly efficient schemes of income redistribution or, in the language of Hicks and Kaldor, income compensation (Hicks 1939; Kaldor 1939).

In one way or another, disguised moral judgments implicit in such utility theorizing may inhere in the claim that people should have, and should be allowed to have, what they prefer. But it may well be possible to argue on good grounds that individual preferences cannot necessarily be taken to be amoral, and that no moral desiderata at all should be adduced in relation to them. The market system may function more or less efficiently, for example, in connection with the supply of and demand for commodities whose existence and use attract, on grounds of ethical judgment, moral opprobrium. Commodities related to activities of vice, such as illegal drug use and pornography, or, to take a recently prominent example, certain types of handguns, provide instances of what is in view. Other examples abound.

Or we may take a case under recent discussion. On the one hand the cigarette manufacturing industry in the United States has come under investigation for the implications of its product for the spread of cancer. Even the deleterious effects of so-called second hand smoke have been investigated and scientifically evaluated. Government offices, domestic airlines, restaurants, universities, and many private offices have been declared smoke-free zones. Yet the tobacco growers who, it has lately been officially claimed, are producing an addictive drug, are the beneficiaries of government price supports, and it has been proposed that a cigarette tax be relied on to provide partial funding of a scheme of national health insurance. Some ethical confusion would appear to be implicit in many of the issues that arise in this connection.

As to individual preference again, rational and effective decision and choice are necessarily dependent on the possession of adequate and relevant information. In many instances in relation to which market systems operate, market participants may not be in possession of that level or degree of information on which good, or best, judgments can be made. The provision of information therefore itself becomes a moral issue, as does the possible supervision and regulation of the dissemination of information. The ethics or morality of advertising, or that of the income tax deductibility of the cost of it, come immediately to issue. Or to take a very different question, the information content of prescription or over-the-counter drug advertising, and also the high retail cost of such items, similarly may raise questions worthy of ethical evaluation. That may be the case, for example, if the high retail price imposed by drug manufacturers purports to provide reimbursement for high research expenditures, when such expenditures may in fact have been financed to some extent by government subsidies in the first place.

THE POSITIVE-NORMATIVE DISTINCTION

The questions raised in this chapter point to that of the necessity, and therefore the possibility, of maintaining a rigid and carefully sanitized distinction between the normative and the positive in economic argument. If, for any of a number of reasons that have been implied, it is impossible to maintain that economics is, always and everywhere, a value-free discipline, then the normative-positive distinction falls to the ground. Positive economics is concerned essentially with questions of how the economic system operates and what results might be expected to follow if actions of certain kinds are taken. It is concerned with what is. Normative economics is concerned with what, against certain established criteria, ought to be. It has to do with the values attached to economic arrangements and institutions and with whether it is to the ends encapsuled in them that economic policies should be, or with ethical propriety can be, directed.

The positive and the normative, it is clear, are frequently commingled in economics (see Hausman and McPherson 1993, 677ff.). Samuelson's well-known paper (1958) that led to extensive work in overlapping generations theory, for example, has had a heavy influence on subsequent theories of money and macroeconomics (see Hoover 1988; Blanchard and Fischer 1989). But its analysis is heavily dependent on the normative assumptions of the efficiency of perfectly competitive markets (see Hausman 1992, ch. 7).

Similarly, normative assumptions inform the work of representatives of the Chicago School of competitive market analysts. Becker's familiar application of economic analytical categories to the explanation of human behavior (1976, 1981), relating, for example, to the family, fertility, marriage, and crime and punishment, instances the methodology. It assumes the ubiquity and determinative relevance of "maximizing behavior . . . [and] the existence of markets that with varying degrees of efficiency coordinate the actions of different participants—individuals, firms, even nations—so that their behavior becomes mutually consistent" (1976, 5). Becker continues, against assumptions that are quite familiar to economic theory and are heavily laden with normative content, to observe that

preferences that are assumed to be stable . . . are defined over fundamental aspects of life, such as health, prestige, sensual pleasure, benevolence, or envy. . . . The assumption of stable preferences provides a stable foundation for generating predictions about responses to various changes. . . . The combined assumptions of maximizing behavior, market equilibrium, and stable preferences, used relentlessly and unflinchingly, form the heart of the economic approach. (1976, 5)

The commingling or the interintrusiveness of the normative and the positive in Becker's extensive work is instanced in his invocation of the utilitarianism of Bentham and his pleasure-pain calculus. He applauds Bentham's application of that calculus to questions of what we "shall" do as well as to what we "ought" to do. Indeed, Bentham, as Becker sees him, "was primarily interested in 'ought' " (1976, 8). "All human behavior," Becker concludes, "can be viewed as involving participants who maximize their utility from a stable set of preferences and accumulate an optimal amount of information and other inputs in a variety of markets" (1976, 14).

Another example can be observed in the work that has issued from the current neo-Marxian revival, where the normative and the positive are heavily intertwined. At its very core the Marxian interest in class and class consciousness is shot through with normative assumptions and propositions. That work, along with its normative content, is in turn fleshed out by an emphasis on the dialectical tensions between the relations of production, or the structure of property ownership and the rules of economic organization, and the forces of production, or the technological arrangements in accordance with which economic production and exchange proceed. Marxian scholarship has lately addressed, albeit against very different analytical presuppositions, issues that engaged Becker in his human behavior studies. The supposed reality of communism within the family or the household, for example, has recently been studied by Fraad, Resnick, and Wolff (1989, 9–69), and the journal *Rethinking Marxism* has accommodated numerous studies on related issues such as gender, race, class, capitalism, accumulation, and theories of value (see also Resnick and Wolff 1985, 1987. See also, for more extensive neo-Marxian analysis, Roemer 1981, 1982, 1985, 1986, 1988, 1994).

The important and prolific work of Sen also instances the difficulties of maintaining an untarnished normative-positive distinction. His essay on "Rational Fools: A Critique of the Behavioral Foundations of Economic Theory" ([1976–77] 1979) strikes at the foundations of a number of neoclassical utility theoretic assumptions. Normativities enter in Sen's proposals that assumptions of sympathy and commitment might well be taken, along with more familiar assumptions of self-interest, to determine human behavior. Commitment, as previously observed, is closely associated with moral and ethical principles, and its entry into economic argument drives a wedge between individual choice and welfare as that has been more commonly understood. In surveying his own agenda Sen concludes that "these questions are connected, of course, with ethics, since moral reasoning influences one's actions, but in a broader sense these are matters of culture, of which morality is one part" (1976–77, reprinted in Hahn and Hollis 1979, 101).

A CONCLUDING EVALUATION

It follows that it is something of a pretense for economists to argue that the normative-positive distinction, which John Neville Keynes, Robbins, Hutchison and others have claimed is necessary and possible, can be preserved. To adapt the title of Caldwell (1982), we are "beyond positivism" or, as Hausman and McPherson observed, beyond "the heyday of positivist methodology." But against that reality two things are to be said.

First, it is not necessary to remain as discouraged about the status and prospects of economics as Joan Robinson seemed to be in her conclusion that "economics limps along with one foot in untested hypotheses and the other in untestable slogans" (1962, 25). What is necessary, undoubtedly, is that in the light of the inevitability of its value-impregnation, economic argument, as Myrdal claimed, should strive consistently to make its values and value judgments explicit and clearly recognizable. That applies to a number of the economist's activities: the selection of fields of study, the conceptualization of research problems and agendas, the methods of enquiry, the interpretation of data and the way in which "facts" are to be understood and defined as relevant, and the behavior criteria or policy proposals that follow.

In the very nature of the case, as has been argued, economics, as both an analytical and a policy oriented discipline, cannot be value-free. The very nature of reasoning in the human sciences, and the nature of decision criteria that affect human behavior, render such a freedom from the tarnishing influence of value presuppositions and orientation both impossible and unnecessary. What can be done is to make explicit at every turn what the economist understands to be the value orientations that structure and determine his or her work, the analytical and practical research design that is involved in it, and the nature of, and the reasons for, the policy proposals to which it gives rise.

Second, the inevitable value-impregnation of economic argument suggests that the unsustainable normative-positive distinction might more usefully be replaced by a different methodological distinction. That is the division between descriptive economics on the one hand and analytical economics, with all its scope for model-building and its assumption content, on the other. But it is important to note at that point that such a classification of the economist's work in no sense escapes, nor is it designed to escape, from the value-impregnation itself. Value judgments remain. But their presence and, moreover, their determinative influence can be recognized on both the descriptive and the analytical levels.

On the level of description, the question of genuine facticity can then be addressed and recognized with clear intellectual comfort and integrity. For example, it will be able to be clearly understood what is the meaning and significance of, or what the investigating economist takes to be the meaning and significance of, the "fact" that workers are idled by involuntary unemployment. Or a similar reaction can be envisaged to the "fact" that retail commodity prices are set where they are as a result, conceivably, of different degrees of market pricing power that monopolistic or oligopolistic producing firms enjoy. Instances can be multiplied.

By the same token, the value orientation of analytical economics, including at that stage the conceivably quite heavy value-loadings implicit in the assumption content of the theory-building, can be more conscientiously articulated. For example, the morality, or perhaps the imagined amorality, of certain behavior assumptions and behavior criteria can be explicitly recognized. The criminal, for example, if he is contemplated in terms of a Becker scheme of thought, might be conceived to think and to act in terms of a trade-off between the expected pay-off from crime and the dangers and potential costs of apprehension. But it is in no sense clear that the economist's legitimate task is discharged simply because he or she has conceptualized a possible utility functional form in terms of which the criminal might proceed. The economic may in no sense be the only, or even the principal, level of determination or causation that is relevant to the criminal's action. The ends in view in the action envisaged might also come within the competence of the economist's critique.

The claim is being made, that is, that the economist qua economist, contrary to Robbins's attempted sanitization of the ends from the means, must inevitably hold in view the value loadings that inhere in both the means and the ends. The economy is not a mere machine, and the economist, along with the worker and every other participant in the economy at every level and stage, is not, and cannot be, and cannot be expected to be, a part of the machinery. Economics takes its place among the intellectual disciplines by recognizing the heavy moral import of the fact that it is a human science, whose objects of investigation are thinking, sentient, acting, and reacting beings. It is an unfortunate but long-lived assumption to the contrary that has informed too much of the conventional development of theory-building, institutional arrangements, and the contemplation of policy options in the subject.

Part III
Issues in Economic
and Ethical Analysis

5   THE ECONOMICS AND ETHICS OF MARKET SUPPLY

In this and the next three chapters we shall put to work in concrete applications the evaluative apparatus that has now been developed. Our focus initially will be on the supply side of the market and on the points at which issues of ethical import arise. The discussion that ensues will take up the twofold and interdependent issues that were raised at the beginning. We shall be concerned at many points, that is, with the question of how the economy works, as well as with the ethical attitudes and determinations that are relevant to it. The first of these questions needs itself to be seen as having ethical relevance and implications. For if, as will be argued, questions of morality and ethical propriety relate to the structure and functioning of the economy, it is necessary to envisage respects in which that structure might be adapted to accord with what ethical requirements are in view.

On the supply side of the market the nature of the producing firm warrants inspection for its accordance with the pressures of economic morality that are deemed to be relevant. The management of the firm on the one hand, and the suppliers of factor inputs, labor and capital, on the other, face complexes of ethical desiderata. The ethic of work, touching, as we suggested earlier, the ethic of contribution as well as that of entitlement, exerts its pressure, as do those of accountability, solidarity, and responsibility. The categories we raised at the beginning, when we suggested their coalescence in a framework of iterative accountability and solidarity, come to expression in observable respects on the supply side of market activity.

FOUR PRELIMINARY POINTS

Accountability

The ethical concept of accountability enters at many points. It is contiguous frequently with the tension between individuality and solidarity. It will spill over from the microeconomic levels addressed in this chapter to that of the economy as a whole. That will be so in connection with the issue of economic justice and the pressing question of the morality content of schemes for the distribution of economic welfare. The importance of the question will permit at this point a single brief anticipation of its wider application.

In his widely cited and influential *Theory of Justice*, Rawls has proposed a scheme of admissible redistributions of economic benefits. Essentially, it contemplates, in the context of Rawls's "justice as fairness," distributions that contribute maximally to the benefit, or at least to the long run expectations, of the least advantaged members of society. An accountability rests upon the more favored members of society, that is, to justify whatever inequalities of income and wealth they enjoy, on the grounds that the disadvantaged are in some sense thereby benefited. What is implicit in Rawls's proposals is that accountability thereby runs from the advantaged to the disadvantaged, but no reciprocal sense exists in which the disadvantaged are required or responsible to account for their positions. The latter can expect, under Rawls's scheme, to benefit from the provision to them of, as it is said, "minimum social goods," without the necessity of accountability for the condition that justifies their entitlement.

In our present context, on the contrary, the ethic of accountability is understood to be reciprocal or generalized. On the level of work and factor input, individuals are seen as subject to an ethic of what we have called contribution. At the level of decision makers in the firm, ethical mandates are confronted that extend beyond those that address simply the maximum economic wealth or benefit of the owners of the firm.

Deontology or Consequentialism

A second preliminary point recalls the possibility that in confronting accountability and responsibility, decision makers on both the input and the output sides of the firm may be guided by what we have referred to as deontological or consequentialist criteria. The goals or objectives of economic action, that is, may weigh more heavily than a sense of duty or obligation. The quality of work on the one side, as distinct from the number of work hours agreed to in labor contracts, and the target of reportable profits on the other, may both be primarily determinative. Different possible conceptions of responsibilities and related decision criteria will be noted in later sections of this chapter.

The Evolution of Market Systems

The ethical problems on these levels have arisen in part, no doubt, from the fact that the invisible hand of Smithian and classical markets has been replaced by the very visible hand of concentrated economic power. Those concentrations of power have occurred in industrial complexes, in the forms of monopolistic and oligopolistic structures, and among the collectivized suppliers of labor. The concentrated power of governments and their market interventions has also exerted its influence. In earlier times the assumptions of individual economic self-interest and freely competitive markets might have been expected to lead to the common good of society. Along the way, the impersonal and automatic harmony of the market system, if, in fact, that harmony could be shown to exist, may have disguised the emerging cleavages between markets and morality.

But those relative simplicities of industrial and production arrangements were soon significantly changed. In his brief but ethically challenging essay on "The Moral Predicament of the Market Economy," Walter Weisskopf has summed up the trends that emerged in the later nineteenth century and their projection into modern times. He laments that "formal, value-empty rationality for its own sake became the moral philosophy of economics." An earlier ethicism, as Weisskopf sees it, was vacated. He pleads for "a reorientation of our economic attitudes and goals under the aegis of social and individual morality" (1977, 37, 40). In the event, an obeisance to the objectives and requirements of the "rational economic man" in economic thought set out to establish a value-free enquiry with only minimal explicit address to ethical priorities.

In later times, tensions have therefore increased between efficiency and ethics, between consumption targets and distributive justice, and between monetary gain and morality. The competitive incisions of social Darwinism, the subjective, materialistic hedonism of the individual, and the economists' commitment to a newer and positivist scientism, have structured and clouded the moral relevance of the subject.

The outcomes that have resulted have troubled evaluators of the economic scene. Buchanan, in a review of the ethical content of economic libertarianism, instanced, for example, by Nozick's *Anarchy, State, and Utopia* (1974), observes that "to assume that the cumulative result of a series of just actions must itself be just is to commit the fallacy of composition" (1985, 68). Nozick, in his recent *The Nature of Rationality*, has withdrawn to some extent from the anarchic implications of his earlier work. He acknowledges that "the political philosophy presented in [the earlier work] ignored the importance to us of . . . our social ties and concern and hence is inadequate" (1993, 32). In doing so, Nozick is linking his earlier "entitlement theory" (1993, 9n.) with considerations of solidarity, in a manner similar to what our own thought forms have proposed. Buchanan has also recognized that a focused concern for maximized individual well-being may well give rise to system-wide outcomes that leave some members of society economically disadvantaged.

In their edited volume on *Markets and Morals*, Dworkin, Bermant, and Brown have observed that

since Hume, philosophers have called attention to the 'logical gap' that separates normative from factual judgments. Formulating social policy requires normative judgments concerning the ends that such policy seeks to attain, the appropriateness of the means used, the type of society we would like to live in, and the values we wish to develop and preserve. (1977, 13)

Economics, in short, is value-laden. Among the ways that might be found to close the philosophers' "logical gap," a responsibility exists to articulate those that reside in "the intersection of economics . . . and moral philosophy" (1977, 13). The "gap," moreover, between the normative and the positive, might very well be seen, it has already been argued, to be ultimately and fundamentally unsustainable.

Economic Conscience

Economists, notwithstanding their fairly general commitment to amorality in economic argument, have invoked, in a somewhat sporadic manner, the significance of conscience as an arbiter of individual behavior. From that direction a sense of obligation or personal responsibility has filtered its influence into economic argument. The latter has thereby acquired a flavor of deontological criteria.

Adam Smith had raised the importance of conscience in the guise of what he referred to as an "impartial spectator" (see Raphael 1975). In doing so he had behind him the Humean tradition of the "judicious spectator" or the external "bystander" and the similar emphases of his teacher Hutcheson. But "what is original in Adam Smith is the development of the concept to explain the judgements of conscience made by an agent about his own actions" (Raphael 1975, 87).

Joan Robinson in more recent times, in a context in which the claims of egoism are set against those of altruism, has spoken of the fact, as she sees it, that the "mechanism by which [the claims of others upon us] are imposed is the moral sense or conscience of the individual" (1962, 5). As to the origin of conscience, however, or the grounding of its dictates, Robinson can only observe that "a propensity to develop a conscience is in the structure of a healthy human brain. It is very similar to the propensity to learn to talk" (1962, 7). Religion or theology, as Robinson explicitly observes, has nothing necessarily to do with conscience or ethical grounding. But at the same time, "reason will not help. The ethical system implanted in each of us by our upbringing . . . was not derived from any reasonable principles" (1962, 12). It seems that here we encounter an ethical intuitionism whose grounding is not in any meaningful sense able to be formalized. In her agnostic attempt to preserve some system and significance in her argument at that point, Robinson concludes with the not very well-substantiated claim that "any economic system requires a set of rules, an ideology to justify them, and a conscience in the individual which makes him strive to carry them out" (1962, 13).

THE NATURE OF THE FIRM

The nature of the firm, with the extent to which it satisfies criteria of economic morality, presents a significant locus at which the preceding issues come to concrete expression. On the level of economic analysis it is possible to question whether the most significant conceptualization of the firm's activities has been achieved in the currently existing forms of industrial and corporate organization. For it is generally understood that, to put it briefly, capital employs labor. This has involved, moreover, the notion that the providers of capital have a right to all the value of what is produced after paying the suppliers of labor a contractual reward for their services. Such a way of looking at things is no doubt consistent with widely accepted forms of industrial and financial capitalism. But it is precisely the rightness or the reasonableness of that assumption that can be called in question, and at least subjected to the need to produce acceptable and ethical vindication.

On the level of pure analysis, it might as well be said that labor employs capital, as that capital employs labor. The contemporary philosopher David Haslett (1994) has recently presented a challenging argument on *Capitalism with Morality*, in which a form of "worker control" is proposed. Putterman (1984) and Weitzman (1983, 1984) have joined the debate. For an international flavor, with reference to Japan where joint capital and labor ventures have come to new prominence, Abegglen and Stalk (1988) and Aoki (1990) are highly relevant. Similarly, experiments with alternative forms of organization of the firm have been introduced in what was previously Yugoslavia (see Putterman 1990). In the latter case, Putterman refers to the Yugoslavian system as "an only half-reformed centralized socialist economy" (1990, 177, quoted in Haslett 1994, 187). In the Yugoslavian system workers owned capital assets collectively, but they did not own individual shares that could be sold, or redeemed for cash, on leaving the enterprise. The latter facility is an important part of what Haslett has proposed as worker control.

If, in the producing firm as it is envisaged in the neoclassical theory, all of the factors of production except one are held to be given and fixed, then the marginal productivity of the other factor can be specified and the criteria of its optimum employment invoked in the familiar manner. But more is involved in fact than any such analytical abstraction. First, the question arises as to who in the industrial structure is legitimately entitled to receive the surplus of the actual values of produced outputs, over and above the contractual payments to whichever factor is considered to be the employed rather than the employer. In that connection the concept of economic exploitation potentially arises. The exploitation of labor by capitalist owners may occur, not necessarily only or exclusively in the sense in which Marx, for example, saw it, if an unfair or morally indefensible system of income distribution exists. Or the legitimate interests of capitalist owners may be exploited by the suppliers of labor if attempts are made to insist on unsustainable wage and salary payments or increases.

Second, it needs to be considered also whether social realities might more properly be served by recognizing that labor and capital are in fact cooperating factors of production, sharing in the risks involved in industrial operations, and entitled, as a result, to shares in the rewards and values that may be realized.

The producing firm, in short, might well be considered a joint venture of cooperating labor and capital. The suppliers of labor and the suppliers of capital can be envisaged as coming together to collaborate in the production of a commodity output which, it is hoped, will provide a return in excess of total costs of production. The objective of the enterprise, in other words, is to produce a surplus of value. Economics, in the large as well as in the small, has always been concerned with precisely that, the production of surplus. In the classical scheme it was the importance of the capitalist class as the providers of savings, capital, and investment that explained their place in the economic system and justified their receipt of the surplus profit. They provided the engine of growth in the economy that was then beginning to enjoy accelerated development. Marx, as is well known, made much of the concept of the surplus, though his conceptualization of surplus labor gave an idiosyncratic twist to the familiar economic concept.

The notion of surplus has continued to engage economists' interest throughout subsequent theoretical development. In the context of the modern firm the notion of the surplus value has acquired a precise meaning. It refers to the value of production that remains after paying not only the contractual rewards to variable factors of production such as labor and paying the cost of acquiring necessary material inputs, but after setting aside also a periodic amount to replace the capital equipment that is used up in the course of production. A surplus remains, that is, after making provision for maintaining capital intact.

But the question arises, on the level of socio-economic justice, as to how the surplus produced in the sense referred to should be distributed. That question takes the argument beyond the more usual analysis based on assumptions as to input magnitudes and the fixity of capital and the variability of labor. What reason exists, it might be asked, why it should be automatically imagined that the providers of capital have a prior claim to the full amount of the surplus? Or what reason exists why the providers of labor should not also share in the distribution of the surplus? If, as has been suggested, the productive enterprise is viewed as a cooperative venture of both labor and capital, then why should not the providers of both factors of production share in the distribution of the surplus that has been generated by their cooperative effort?

Or to put the proposition in another way, it might well be imagined that the providers of capital are entitled to a rate of return on their investment that is in some sense normal, or perhaps higher than is available on risk-free investments by a margin that is a reasonable compensation for risk bearing. Then the surplus remaining after that rate of return on capital has been paid, and after the necessary provision for the maintenance of capital intact has also been made, might be distributed between the providers of both labor and capital.

It could be claimed, of course, that the providers of capital bear all the risks and that they should therefore receive all of the surplus return. But that, surely, hardly fits the facts. For it would strain credulity to conclude that the suppliers of labor are in no sense risk bearers. First, the suppliers of labor have a definite interest in the long run survival of the firm, particularly in cases where they have made investments in developing personal and possibly highly specialized skills that are not easily transferable to other uses and employments. Second, labor in general is clearly exposed to the vicissitudes of cyclical economic fluctuations that impose upon it a prospective instability in earnings quite akin to the fluctuations in rates of return on invested capital.

It may be thought that in the event of a decline in the prosperity of a firm or in its prospects for longer run survival, the money capital funds invested in it may be lost and gone for ever, while the suppliers of labor can transfer their effort to other lines of employment. But such an argument might well be precisely the opposite of the facts in any number of cases. It may be true that real capital may have a realizable value that is quite low if the attempt is made to transfer it to other lines of employment. Capital that begins its life as putty may very quickly turn to clay, and it may be so specialized to a particular use that it is not effectively transferable at all. In other terms, the realizable monetary value of real capital, in the absence of ready spot markets for second hand real capital assets, may be minimal. For those reasons, the suppliers of capital are undoubtedly risk bearers in a very real sense. But on the other hand, judicious capital management may well make money capital realizable and transferable by such devices as corporate mergers, horizontal or vertical integration, marginal technological change and development, and by product design and redesign. The same result may be achieved by the marketability on recognized stock exchanges of the claims to corporate assets, or the shares of common stock that represent the ownership of the firm in the conventional sense.

While all that is so, the suppliers of labor are undoubtedly risk bearers in a very real sense also. For contrary to the assumption that has just been made, their services may not be transferable at all. Labor skills may be as highly specialized as real capital assets, and alternative employment opportunities might in no sense readily abound. Moreover, considerable costs may well be incurred by the suppliers of labor, such as dislocation or relocation costs and capital losses on housing investment when relocation becomes necessary, quite apart from the social and psychic costs of cultural disturbances. For all such reasons it may be quite wide of the mark to conclude that only capital, and not labor, can be regarded as a risk-bearing factor of production.

To the extent that cogency inheres in these arguments, there is every reason why labor and capital should share, not only in the distribution of earned surplus in the manner that can thus be contemplated, but also in the management of the enterprise. That would seem to be the case when the enterprise is regarded, in ways that have been implied, as in every sense a joint venture between capital and labor. For considerations of economic and social justice argue that the suppliers of labor should have a share in the determination of industrial policies that bear so vitally on their prospects for economic and socio-cultural well-being.

It has been claimed that when the suppliers of labor are accorded a share or a voice in enterprise management a loss of flexibility and efficiency may result. It might not then be possible, it has been argued, to achieve the variations in the level of employment in the firm that will accord it the best prospects of weathering cyclical fluctuations in economic activity or the technological changes that become necessary from time to time. That may be so to a greater or lesser extent. But that very argument points as much to the need to establish working procedures to meet such contingencies as it does to the issues of morality that are involved.

All such questions, it will be clear, open avenues to the consideration of ethical behavior in the exploitation or otherwise of labor in individual firms. Or, as we put it at the beginning of this discussion, linkages are thereby opened between market activity in general and the rightness or otherwise of institutional arrangements that bear on the welfare of the economy at large.

If, as is proposed, the firm is to be understood as a joint production activity in which the suppliers of all factors of production share in responsibility, risks, rewards, and losses, two questions arise. First, in what form should the suppliers of labor, for example, acquire an ownership interest in the firm? And second, in what manner should such ownership interests be vested, or redeemable, or transferable in monetary value terms if and when employment in the firm is terminated?

These questions are answerable in at least two possible ways. First, normal contractual employment and wage contracts can contemplate the progressive acquisition of ownership shares as a part of regular annual remunerations. The opportunity to acquire such shares could be related in a mutually agreed sense, and at possibly differential rates, to the length of employment in the firm. In that event, the monetary value of the ownership that is thus acquired would depend on the share values at any specific date as reflected in stock exchange quotations. Values at employment termination dates would thus be readily assessable. Or in the absence of stock exchange quotations, in the case, perhaps, of more closely held corporations, agreements regarding termination values of ownership shares could be written into employment contracts in the first place. Such termination values, of course, would depend on the economic position and prospects of the firm at that time. But that very statement illustrates again the initial concept that the suppliers of labor, as well as the traditionally understood suppliers of capital, are in very real senses risk bearers in the firm. The rates at which such employee ownership share distributions are valued at the time of allocation would depend on the manner in which, as indicated already, a part of the firm's annual income was allocated to the suppliers of labor after paying all production costs and providing the depreciation reserve necessary to maintain the firm's real capital investment intact.

Alternatively, employment contracts could specify that nominal bonus points were to be accumulated by employees for each year of their service, related again in an agreed fashion to levels of wage remuneration, length of service, employee grade or classification, and productivity achievements. At the agreed upon bonus point allocation dates each year a monetary value, determined in a manner similar to the foregoing, could be placed on the points allocation for that year. That valuation would depend again on the economic status and prospects of the firm. At the same time, previously accumulated points could be revalued, and putative capital gains or losses could be imputed to them on the basis of historic outcomes and prospective economic trends. Under such conditions, the total amount of the firm's net income that was available for bonus point distribution each year would depend, as before, on the initially established rules of income sharing. The termination or the redeemable value of employee ownership shares could again proceed in similar terms.

THE ETHIC OF WORK OR CONTRIBUTION

On the supply side of the market, ethical issues arise on a number of more detailed levels. Prominent among them is the ethic of work and the structure of and degree of compliance with employment contracts.

The ethic of work did not await, of course, the emergence of market structures that followed the demise of the medieval manorial or feudal

system. The breakdown of the medieval system, the enclosure movements, the expanding technologies, international exploration and trade,
and the newer forms and expressions of nationalism gave rise to the emergence of labor as a more or less mobile factor of production. As a result,
a uniquely recognizable market for labor developed. But the ethic of work
did not ensue only from those developments. It did not await the libera-
tion of the individual and the rediscovery of individual dignity and prerogatives that formed a principal deposit of the Reformation. Adam in the
Garden of Eden anticipated Adam Smith in understanding the work of
hunting beaver and deer. For even if, in that pristine environment,
resources were not scarce in their subsequent sense, time itself unfolded
at its own rate and the original Adam could do only one thing at any one
time. It would conceivably take different amounts of time to do different
things and complete different tasks.

But if the ethic of work is as old as creation, widely different degrees of
commitment to it have informed the process of economic activity and
development. In analytical terms, the ethic is in no sense properly discharged by the neoclassical notion that the suppliers of labor maximize a
utility function defined over the real wage rate and the leisure chosen from
the 24 hour day. The nicely calculated less or more as expressed in the concept of the marginal rate of substitution between income and leisure, and
the equality of that with the slope of the boundary of a choice set defined
by a wage rate line, does not say all that needs to be said about the ethics
of labor supply. For any conception of the utility function, against which a
supplier of labor optimizes his or her position, may well contain other arguments. In the same way as we observed previously that Sen's behavior
functions may have regard to sympathy and commitment as well as to individual self-interest, so now in the matter of the supply of labor other arguments might well need to be introduced.

A distinction needs to be drawn between the wage contract that
employers and workers establish on the one hand, and, on the other, the
intensity of effort or the integrity, not to say the skill and competence, with
which work effort is supplied in the workplace. At issue at that point, also,
is the question of supervision and administration costs that are imposed on
industry by the different possible ways in which work effort is managed
and supplied.

The literature on efficiency wage models, incentive payments, and
bonus motivations attests the relevance to industrial costs and consequent
product pricing that ensues in these connections (see Mankiw and Romer
1991, 2:111–243). For the quality of work effort, in all too many respects,
cannot be encapsuled and defined in employee wage contracts. That being
so, it follows that greater or lesser commitment to work obligations, or
firmer or looser regard for the ethic of work responsibilities, pushes to
higher or lower levels the cost of production of industrial output. It is a

short step to observe that market prices, which will in general be set by producing firms at a level necessary to provide a target or desired rate of return on invested capital, will be affected as a result. That in turn will have traceable implications more generally for social welfare and benefit. It is in that connection that analytical economics has established the concept, not simply of the money wage, but the so-called efficiency wage, or the effective wage per unit of effort actually supplied and obtained.

In the language of the meta-ethical categories we have reviewed, individual suppliers of work effort will decide whether their ethical motivation derives from a deontological, or obligatory, or a teleological or consequentialist premise. There is undoubtedly a sense in which the preceding argument raises the implicit importance of more than a consequentialist ethical criterion. Work and work satisfaction presumably hinge on more than the objective of economic reward. Issues of self-fulfillment and the sense of obligation that integrity of effort demands are relevant and exert their impact. They affect production costs and market prices and they bear on achievable standards of more generalized economic well-being.

The ethic of employer-employee relations takes on, also, somewhat larger dimensions. Consider again an issue that bears in some respects on the critical and no doubt highly emotive question of economic exploitation. In the industrial nexus, exploitation may occur at any of a number of levels. Employers may in various ways exploit the employed, for example in the writing of wage contracts, the establishment of work rules, and the exercise of asymmetric bargaining power. Industrial corporations, in the exercise of monopolistic or oligopolistic market and pricing power, may exploit consumers in the interest of achieving higher than normal, or what is in some sense reasonable, rates of return on capital. Or again, consumers may be exploited by dishonest or unsustainable advertising and quality claims that influence market consumption patterns. At the same time, conditions may arise in which the suppliers of labor may exploit to their advantage the employing industrial firms, and they may thereby in due course exploit the consuming public. Such a condition may arise if a concentration of economic power in the hands of the suppliers of labor or their representatives leads to an insistence on increases in wage rates in excess of the ability of the economy to pay such increases.

That possible development may in turn have generalized implications for economic stability on a system-wide scale with, again, aggregative welfare implications. For what has just been termed the ability of the economy to make increased income payments, meaning thereby incomes of all kinds and not only or simply hourly paid wage rates, depends on the rate at which industrial productivity can be, or is being, increased. For if, in short, the annual rate of increase in income payments is greater than the simultaneous rate of increase in industrial productivity, then an upward pressure on industrial production costs and market prices can be expected to result.

Or in sharper terms, that condition follows if the rate of increase in the reward per unit of labor is greater than the rate of increase in the average rate of productivity per unit of labor. It is at that point that the possibility of a cost-induced inflation arises.

The problem of exploitation that is thus capable of entering the industrial nexus can be put in other terms. It emerges as an attempt on the part of different classes of income earners to increase their shares of the national income and production, to the disadvantage of other classes. The question that is here implied, that of achieving an equitable distribution of the shares in the national product, raises quite clearly the large issue of distributive justice. We shall return to that at more length.

PROPERTY RIGHTS AND ECONOMIC USE

In the market system as it is here addressed, morality claims arise forcibly in connection with the sanctity of property, the rightness of private ownership claims to it, and the prerogatives of its economic employment. The concept of property includes the right of property in personal, individual labor and the legitimate prospects of reward for its use. It includes also both personal and real property. Property in general and comprehensive terms, then, is seen as having a moral value in itself. In the various cases to be considered, appeal can be made to the fundamental notion of the moral value of equal respects for persons and their inherent rights. It may be imagined, of course, that a social Darwinist defense of the market system legitimately adds to the property argument the assumed ethical propriety of the survival of the fittest, or of the fittest, that is, for competition in every relevant economic sense. But if such a social Darwinist argument is accepted, or if such a consequentialist or teleological criterion is held, it would still be necessary, even if difficult, to identify clearly and unarguably its normative content or justification.

It is true that market systems may well develop desirable human traits of independence, industriousness, imagination, and self-discipline. Such characteristics, moreover, as well as the scope for the development of them and the rewards they may realize, may be accorded some ethical justification. But equally, market systems might also develop avarice, greed, duplicity, and insensitivity to others. In the latter sense, they then offend against such criteria as some earlier authors, for example Smith, have advanced. They may ignore, that is to say, the possible ethical significance of what Smith saw as sympathy and fellow-feeling, or, as Sen again proposed, commitment and sympathy as opposed to a severe and rigorously held self-interest. In other words, while it is true that such negative outcomes may carry along with them the achievement of higher levels of productivity and aggregate output, the cost in the form of sacrificed ethical benefits may not be worthwhile or may be morally unjustified.

To the extent that doubt is cast on the moral probity of the capitalist market system as it is most generally known, it does not follow that alternative systems of economic organization necessarily dominate the market system in order of desirability. What is at issue is the comparison, not, for example, between socialism and market capitalism as ideal forms, but between the observable and operating characteristics of each. It may reasonably be judged that what has been referred to at several points as the tension between individuality and solidarity can be satisfactorily resolved, from the point of view of moral import, within a suitably structured capitalist market system. In those respects, Buchanan's critique to which we have already referred can usefully be set against Haslett's conception of the mixed economy (1994, 187). In other terms, the arguments that stem from the neo-Marxian revival (Resnick and Wolff 1985, 1987) can be set against those of Keynes in his *General Theory* (1936). Keynes, as a calm reading of his work makes clear, was concerned to save capitalism, not to replace it.

In these several ways claims arise, in the context of ethical justification, for the sanctity of property in real and personal assets and skills, for the responsibility, prerogatives, and accountability of individual behavior, and for more generalized welfare or a solidarity that looks to the interests of society in the large. It is the resolution of tensions that arise on those levels that connotes the important ethical dilemmas.

It has been acknowledged that in perfectly uninhibited, freely functioning market activity, both commodity demands and supplies may be channeled onto the production of things that might in themselves be thought to be morally condemnable. That possibility addresses from another perspective the ethical inviolability of what were seen above as property rights and the right of the economic exercise of them. It is clear that judicious consideration can properly be given in any number of cases to the regulation of the exercise of such property rights in the interests of satisfying higher, or, from the point of view of social and cultural acceptability, more widely conceived ethical and moral standards and criteria. At the same time, of course, room may well exist for differences of view among persons of goodwill on some such levels. In the case, as referred to earlier, of the possible regulation of the cigarette manufacturing industry, differences of view may exist as to the reliability of the supposed scientific conclusion that tobacco is carcinogenic, or that nicotine is addictive. Differences of judgment may therefore exist regarding the extent to which, as a result, social intervention in the production and distribution of tobacco products is ethically acceptable.

Moreover, standards of moral judgment in such an instance may themselves be historically and culturally determined. As a result of scientific advance, for example, what might have been considered culturally acceptable some decades ago, tobacco use for example, might be looked upon with opprobrium today.

The ethics of personal property entitlements and of the free and uninhibited use of property raises two further questions that are worthy of
economists' consideration. First, as Rawls has argued (1971, 136–41,
251–57, referenced in Buchanan 1985, 69), it may be necessary to envisage
the need in certain circumstances for societal action to restrict what might
otherwise be a fuller use of private property. That might be thought necessary in order to compensate, possibly through schemes of income or wealth
redistribution, disadvantaged individuals whose initial economic endowments are so slender as to curtail their opportunities for effective participation in the economic process. What is at issue in that case is the moral
acceptability of each individual's starting point in the economic process.
While it is ethically unnecessary to envisage, or for that matter impossible
to achieve and maintain, strict economic equality across all members of
society, at least the provision of equality of opportunity can be ethically
endorsed. That equality of opportunity may well call for institutional
action designed to redress previously existing and inherited disadvantages.

Moral sanction, therefore, may exist in cases in which accidents of inheritance produce a significant inequality of wealth distribution. Economists,
as a result, justifiably struggle with the question of the ethical propriety of
inheritance and estate taxation that might be employed to iron out some of
the more highly skewed inequalities. It has been argued to the contrary by
those of libertarian persuasion, such as Nozick in his earlier work, that
while such inequalities of wealth distribution might be economically unfortunate, the inviolable sanctity of private property prevents the accusation
that such distributions are unjust, provided only that no person's private
property rights have been violated. Such a libertarian perspective may propose that the disadvantaged might benefit from the moral duty of those
better off to be charitable. But it is claimed also from that perspective that
the less well off have no unarguable right to economic aid. A clash occurs,
however, between economic justice on the one hand and charity or benevolence on the other. That clash is instanced by only a minimal reflection on
the fact of, and the reasons for, the poor laws throughout British history,
and the attempts at the provision of welfare and the ensuing proposals for
welfare reform since the 1930s in the United States.

The ethic of charitableness may be embraced from the viewpoint of a
sense of obligation, and in that sense be deontic. But it has frequently been
pointed out that questions of so-called free rider problems and problems of
assurance stand in the way of the effectiveness of charity as a means of
addressing socio-economic disadvantages. The free rider problem refers to
the fact that one might easily be discouraged from charitable activities, particularly those that require the surrender of tangible wealth, if it is thought
that other members of society will be reluctant to contribute in a similar
fashion. One may be fearful, that is, that one's charitable contributions may

simply make it possible for other individuals to enjoy a free ride, or to allow their social consciences to be alleviated by other people's actions. The question of assurance refers to the fact that one may be disinclined to contribute to charitable causes unless he or she has an assurance that others will do likewise. In either case, reasons that argue on such grounds for individual non-participation clearly diminish the projected effectiveness of charity as a means to the end of improved social justice (see Buchanan 1985, chap. 3).

Milton Friedman, prominently among those who argue for the sanctity of civil and political liberties, has seen the market as the best protector of those rights (1962). But again, the dispersion of power that competitive markets are thought capable of achieving will not necessarily guarantee everywhere economic liberty and, as was observed above, everywhere equality of opportunity. For it is apparent that industrial and financial capitalism as it has developed has led to high concentrations of economic power. It can be argued also that those concentrations of power have been exploited to the disadvantage of some members of society. That may be accomplished, as we have already noted, as a result of asymmetric bargaining power as between employer and employed, or through monopolistic or oligopolistic pricing policies. Or it may result from the control over sources of materials, tied outlet dealerships, and the less than ethical exploitation of, for example, long term, cost-plus, government contracts.

Ethical desiderata impact also on access to education, and on the discrimination that might or might not be associated with it, as that is relevant to equality of opportunity. Questions of the fairness of educational facilities arise among different population segments, social classes, and geographical areas. In the last-named case, different degrees of development may have led to differences of cultural opportunities or deprivation. Economic institutions designed to redress any number of such inequities may therefore be contemplated.

THE ETHICS OF PARETO OPTIMALITY

A further respect in which the question of property and its distribution is ethically relevant has to do with what we referred to as individuals' starting points in the economic process. Consider for this purpose what has been referred to analytically as Pareto-optimum distributions. We may envisage a pair of individuals, or a set of individuals, engaged in production and trade, and we may focus for the moment on the resulting distribution of commodity outputs among them.

Any such distribution is said to be Pareto optimal if it is not possible to envisage any other distribution that would make one individual better off without at the same time making at least one other individual worse off.

Leaving aside at this point the possibilities of coalitions of trading individuals and the movement of the trading system to what has been labeled its core (analytically a definable subset of trading points on an Edgeworthian contract curve), it can be demonstrated that efficiently functioning, perfectly competitive markets lead, under well-defined conditions, to Pareto-optimum results. Those conditions include such assumptions as the availability of full information as to all aspects of market and trading opportunities; rational individuals in the sense that certain axioms of behavior, such as transitivity of preferences, are satisfied; the absence of transactions costs and costs of enforcing contracts; homogeneous products in specific markets; freedom of entry to and exit from markets; and the absence of externalities. But of course, the extent to which actual markets approximate such ideal arrangements or requirements varies, and empirical deviations from the ideal can be readily observed.

Nevertheless, the notion of the Pareto optimum, which implies essentially, it will be clear, a concept of economic efficiency, has been extensively employed in economic and market analysis. It has been allowed, first, to establish a conceptual benchmark against which actual market outcomes can be evaluated. Second, it has been allowed to suggest that Pareto-optimum outcomes, to the extent that they are observed or approximated, establish the ethical justification for market functioning and results.

But from the point of view of moral justification it has to be recognized that the Pareto-optimum outcome, to use at this point a relevant technical term, is not distribution-free. By that it is meant that the Pareto-optimum point at which trading individuals arrive, as defined in the foregoing sense, depends on the points from which they started. It depends, in other words, on the initial distribution of resources, or income or wealth endowments, with which the individuals entered the economic production and trading process. If, again, those initial distributions had been different, the parties to the market transactions would necessarily have reached a point that satisfied the Pareto-optimum conditions at a different distribution of outputs. Where one ends up in the economic process depends very much, that is, on the point from which one starts. It is in the sense in which the end result depends on the wealth or income or resource distributions at the starting points that the Pareto optimum is said to be not distribution-free.

The implication of that analytical argument for our present purposes is simply that morality attaches to one's estimate of the acceptability of the initial distribution of endowments in the economy. Again we are returned to the issue of the status, as to their opportunities for effective economic participation and their sharing in the benefits of what the economy produces, of different individuals, economic and social classes, and inhabitants of geographical areas. Raised at this ethically significant point, therefore, is the larger question of the morality of income and wealth distribution to which we shall return.

THE ETHICS OF ENTERPRISE MANAGEMENT

In contemplating at this stage the management procedures within the business firm, issues of morality project their imperatives on the levels of both private or individual benefit and the larger social good. Management responsibility extends, that is, to the objective of the economic benefit of the owners of the firm, or the maximization in the shorter or longer run of the economic value of their investment, and, in a number of ways, to responsible social conduct. Enterprise managements confront issues of morality that project again either deontic or consequentialist ethical criteria.

In the development of the joint stock corporation, whose ownership shares are for the main part listed and traded on recognized stock exchanges, a clear separation of ownership from management has frequently emerged. In many instances the ownership shares may be held by investment institutions that do not as a rule interfere with management decisions. Institutional investors may in general prefer to register their displeasure with management decisions by selling their security holdings and rearranging their investment portfolios. That separation of ownership and management places the firm's decision makers in what is essentially a fiduciary position.

The money capital needed to finance the firm's operations is obtainable from debt capital as well as equity or common stock capital sources. In that case the firm's management also has a fiduciary responsibility to the providers of debt capital. That is so in the sense that a responsibility exists to conduct the activities of the firm in such a way as to preserve the prospects that the contractual interest payments on the debt capital will be able to be made. The need exists also to provide the means of repaying the face amount of the debt on its maturity date. The rate of return on ownership capital, which will determine the market value of the ownership stock and therefore the marketability and the liquidity of it, will need to approximate the rate of return required by the owners. It will be calculated after paying the cost of employing all factors of production, including a provision for the replacement of fixed capital assets when they reach the end of their economic lives, and after paying interest on the firm's debt capital.

Issues of morality lie on the surface of all these possible arrangements. First, the recognition of the fiduciary position of the firm's management points to a deontic conception of relevant ethical criteria. For immediately, a sense of obligation is raised by the realities in view. Of course, to the extent that the members of the management, of either its operating and executive management or its board of directors, are also shareholders in the firm, to that extent the decision makers are functioning directly in their own interest. They may, in that situation, confront conditions of conflict of interest, and it is for that reason that laws have been established to prevent, and where necessary to penalize, what is referred to as insider trading in the corporation's ownership shares. Such laws are intended to prevent the management from exploiting other owners of the common stock, by using privileged information they have about the activities, intentions, or prospects of the firm. Such an exploitation may occur if the management uses its privileged information to permit capital gains to be made from buying or selling ownership shares at market prices which will be beneficially changed when the privileged information becomes publicly known. The point at which ethical considerations become crucial, therefore, is that at which decisions are made as to whose interests are primarily at stake in the exercise of management responsibilities.

Second, ethical considerations arise in relation to the firm's operating decisions. These have to do with both internal operations and external economic impacts. On the first of these levels, the fiduciary relationship of the management to the owners imposes criteria of integrity in decisions regarding the employment of productive factors, the cost at which they are acquired, and the fullest possible realization of economic efficiency in the conduct of the firm's operations. In the matter of factor rewards, the rates at which Chief Executive Officers of large corporations are remunerated by their boards of directors might in some cases be difficult to justify on any reasonable grounds of equity or economic necessity. What might have been thought to be over-remuneration in that direction, and the exploitation of privileged management positions associated with it, is clearly observable in, for example, the history in the later 1980s of the United States' Savings and Loan Association industry.

As to internal management decisions, ethical propriety arises in connection with advertising and product promotion. The obligations imposed by the need for truth in advertising are no doubt in themselves clear. False claims as to either product quality or the effectiveness of a commodity in achieving the purposes for which it is marketed clearly offend canons of honesty. But other economic considerations are also at issue in that respect. For in the first place, a responsibility of trust in relation to the external consumer market arises; and secondly, canons of honesty and fairness are violated when unsustainable claims on such levels are made with the objective of favorably influencing the rate of return that can be generated on investment in the firm.

Issues of ethical import arise also, with wider social implications, in connection with the spoliation of the environment and the ecological damage that may result from the firm's operations. Water and air pollution by manufacturing plants, the raping of landscapes by mining operations, the tensions that arise between economic development and the preservation of historic ecological conditions and wildlife habitats, and the question of compensation for damage inflicted on private property, are only instances of a wider range of concern. They all raise issues that propel both economic and ethical considerations.

But all of the issues that have been raised in the preceding paragraphs converge on a single point of ethical significance. The decision makers in the firm are required to decide, that is, what kinds of ethical criteria are to guide their actions, and to take account of the morality content of the ends or management objectives they embrace.

ETHICS AND RISK-BEARING

Ethical considerations, as they are relevant to management action in the firm, bear also on the nature of risks in economic enterprise activity, the reasons why and the extent to which managements undertake differing degrees of risk, and the nature of the responsibilities that are thereby involved.

Analytical economics, to the extent that it has departed from the widely held assumption of full and perfect knowledge, has recognized that the magnitudes of future-dated variables that affect economic outcomes and that enter into the making of decisions cannot be known with certainty. That recognition of uncertainty has introduced risk analysis into economic argument. But for the main part, economists have addressed that reality by assuming that the magnitudes of future-dated variables can be understood as random variables, describable by subjectively assigned probability distributions. At that point the probability calculus has been accorded an entry to economic analysis, and the relevant mathematical statistical apparatus has been imported from the natural sciences in a manner analogous to the importation of a wide range of mathematization in general. But the logical difficulties in the way of maintaining such a procedure derive from the fact that economic decisions, as noted at the beginning, are necessarily made under conditions of ignorance and uncertainty in real historical time.

To the extent that economic argument has assumed that risk can be probabilistically interpreted, a number of assumptions that derive from classic utility theory enter the scheme of things. The extensive literature that is relevant to decision making under conditions of risk as thus understood has generally assumed that a decision maker's expected utility function can be defined over the mathematical moments of the assigned probability distribution of outcomes. A very widely adopted assumption is that of the so-called "mean-variance" analysis, which assumes that expected utility can be defined over the mean and the variance of the probability density function of possible outcomes (see Tobin 1958). Where the partial derivative of such a function with respect to the risk argument, described by the variance of the distribution, is negative, the function is taken to be a "risk aversion" utility function. The degree of risk aversion, then, or the implicit magnitude at different possible utility positions of the marginal rate of substitution between risk and expected rate of return, provides an indication of desired or subjectively acceptable investment prospects and the attractiveness of different possible courses of action.

Against that analytical background, a number of points of entry appear for ethical considerations. First, if, in spite of the epistemological-methodological objections that were earlier raised to the use of the probability calculus, the kind of utility analysis that has just been referred to is adopted, the question arises as to whose utility function is relevant and usable in enterprise management decisions. What responsibility exists, for example, for the management decision makers to ascertain the nature of the risk-return trade-offs that are acceptable to the owners of the firm? Or what, more pointedly, is the possibility that any meaningful attempt could be made to ascertain such an acceptable trade-off? For if, in the case of widely held and publicly traded shares of common stock, the owners are economically diverse, no readily understandable meaning can possibly attach to the owners' utility function, or to such a concept as, in some sense, the average risk-return trade-offs that are acceptable to the owners.

In fact, the best that might be able to be said is that the management's risk-aversion utility function serves as a proxy for that of the owners. That leaves aside, however, the question of how a utility function of a group of management decision makers can be defined, and whose specific risk aversion preferences then come into play in the enterprise decisions. But in any such case the owners, it could be argued, will agree with the decision outcomes of the management, based on whatever utility function is employed, and they will accordingly hold their ownership stock in anticipation of the favorable earnings stream that will result. Or alternatively, if the owners observe management decisions that appear to violate their own risk-return utility preferences, they can register their disapproval by selling the stock. In such a manner, it might be imagined, the financial asset market does achieve, in its trading in shares of corporate common stock, a distribution of ownership, or a clientele, that brings into convergence the preferences as to risk bearing of both corporate managements and the stockholders of the firm.

But it is at the same time true that significant divergences may exist between the risk preferences of the owners and those of the enterprise management. For a holder of common stock can achieve, at least theoretically and to a large extent in fact, any desired level of risk in relation to expected return by combining different firms' common stocks in a diversified asset portfolio. By that means the advantages of diversification may imply that a divergence exists between the risk exposure of a specific firm whose common stock is held and the risk exposure of the investor's portfolio of which it is a part.

The ethical considerations that enter from such directions as these hark back to what was earlier observed as the enterprise management's fiduciary responsibility. They have to do with the management's conception of the stewardship over resources that has been entrusted to it by virtue of the structure of the corporate enterprise. At that point the management may or may not aim at the achievement of the maximum attainable rate of return on the firm's operations. It may consider the wisdom of sacrificing near term or short term gains in the interest of investment in projects that have a longer gestation period and promise more advantageous and possibly more stable returns in the longer run. In doing that, of course, the question arises of the management's ability to make meaningful decisions or estimates regarding outcomes that lie in the more distant future. As is frequently observable in financial asset markets, such a sacrifice of short term profit for longer term gain may lead to hostile take-over bids for the firm's ownership stock. Further, the target rate of return that is adopted may again be evaluated in the light of the risks or uncertainties surrounding the possibility of its realization. In the general case, investment projects or corporate asset structures that imply a higher degree of risk will also offer the prospects of higher rates of return. But it may be judged that certain risk levels lie beyond established limits of acceptability.

Moreover, it has been argued that the utility function in terms of which the management sets out to optimize its decisions if, as has been noted, such a procedure is adopted, may well contain arguments in addition to expected or desired rate of return and risk. The literature spawned by Williamson's early work (1964) has suggested that corporate managers may set as their objective such targets as the size of the firm, the rate of growth and its market share, the size of staff that is supervised, or, as Monsen and Downs suggested, "managers [may] act so as to maximize their own lifetime incomes" (1965, 225; see also Osborne 1964; Leibenstein 1960; Marris 1964; Baumol 1967). Corporate managements may set as their objectives the achievement of power, prestige, socio-cultural influence, or other elements of subjective satisfaction. Such utility function arguments point again to the consideration of the manner in which a responsibility to the owners of the firm, as well as to the suppliers of the several factors of production employed, is recognized and discharged.

A recognition of ethical responsibility at that point does not necessarily imply that low levels of risk will be undertaken, or that risk levels of any specific magnitude will necessarily be adopted. What is at issue is simply that an awareness of economic stewardship will in general prevent the corporate management from acting primarily or consistently in their own best interests as that might be subjectively or selfishly interpreted. They will consider the stability, the growth, and the long run viability of the firm. That calls for operating decisions to be made with the interests in view, not only of the management itself, but also of the workforce, the ownership stock holders, and the possibility of wider social and economic welfare.

AN ECONOMIC EXAMPLE

The prudential management of economic resources and the ethical mandates that are associated with it came forcibly to the public's awareness in the United States as a result of what we noted previously as the crisis in the Savings and Loan Association industry in the 1980s. As a result of the deregulation of the financial sector that followed from the Depository Institutions Deregulation and Monetary Control Act of 1980 and the Garn-St. Germain Act of 1982, the Savings and Loan Associations were permitted to expand their asset investment portfolios beyond the real estate mortgages, principally residential mortgages, in which they had traditionally invested. Not only were loans expanded into commercial real estate ventures that in some instances led to an oversupply of such properties, but loans were made for a wide range of other purposes. In the outcome, what emerged in retrospect as highly irresponsible risk taking by Savings and Loan Association managements led to a widespread bankruptcy and collapse of the Savings institutions. In some cases the collapse was associated with fraudulent management activities and improper uses of shareholders' funds for private purposes. The failure of ethical probity in many such instances can be readily inspected.

In the case of the Savings and Loan Association industry, a further and important consideration enters. That has to do with a failure of responsibility and wisdom on the part of the authors of the deregulation legislation. For at that time there was created what economists have referred to as a moral hazard. Savings and Loan Association managements, in the light of the terms and provisions of the legislation, were actually given an incentive and a motivation to take those excessive risks that led ultimately to the collapse of the industry. For at the same time as the investment prerogatives of the institutions were expanded, the savings funds deposited in the institutions were insured against loss. A government guarantee that depositors would be protected, up to an amount of $100,000 in any one savings account, meant that managements could proceed to make any investments within their legal mandate, of any degree of risk, with the knowledge that their depositors would be protected against possible failure. It was that development that led to the very high cost of resolving the failures that resulted. It led also, as a result, to the large burden that was imposed on the federal government budget, or the burden borne by the taxpayer. That burden became necessary in order to rescue and rehabilitate not only the institutions, a number of which were sold by the responsible government agency at deflated values or were merged with other more viable institutions, but also the large numbers of savers whose funds had been placed in the savings associations.

CONCLUSION

The issues that have been raised in this chapter have addressed the question of ethical proprieties as they relate to actions and decisions on the supply side of market activity. Further questions of resource allocation are affected also by behavior on the demand side of the market, and by what it is, or what it might be, that reflects on the ethical propriety of consumer decisions. For it has been suggested already that issues of morality inhere in what it is that the resources of the economy are devoted to producing, as well as in the processes by which that production is achieved.

Morality attaches also to the rightness or otherwise of the distribution of the rewards and the benefits that productive activity makes possible. In turning in the following chapters to consider a number of those further issues it will be necessary to address at more length the more comprehensive question of what became known as utilitarianism and its expression in economic argument. In addressing that issue note will be taken of a pointedly consequentialist or substantially teleological ethic.

6 UTILITARIANISM AND MARKET DEMAND

The preceding discussion of market supply has questioned the adequacy and the ethical sustainability of a sole reliance on consequentialist criteria. The suppliers of inputs to economic production and the management decision makers in the firm both face complexes of ethical desiderata. Discussion in this chapter of the demand side will raise again from newer perspectives the morality or otherwise of a consequentialist ethic. That ethic, so far as it informs the theory of utility and consumer demand, emerges uniquely from the implications of the philosophy and economics of utilitarianism.

We shall take note in this chapter of the two issues we have held in relationship throughout; namely, the way in which the economy has been understood to work, and the motivation and criteria by which the relevant economic action is guided.

THE CLASSICAL PHILOSOPHIC AND THEORETIC BEQUEST

In the hands of the economic classicists, in the tradition of Ricardo's severe deductivism and a priorism, the assumption of rational behavior in one's own best interest became an integral part of the analysis. Many aspects of analysis were informed by the cold calculations of the rational economic man. They included the Smithian variation of market prices around natural prices; the augmentation of the wage fund as a result of capitalists' saving out of profit income; the Ricardian constraint of diminishing marginal productivity of capital and labor in the wage good industries, notably agriculture; the Malthusian population doctrine that precipitated the iron law of wages; Senior's notion of the abstinence theory of the rate of interest; and the migration of economic resources in search of profit opportunities.

The hegemonic place of the fictional economic man was consolidated by the newer emphases on the demand side of the market that heralded the so-called marginalist revolution in the 1870s. It is clear, of course, that the theory of the margin did not have to wait for the seminal contributions of Jevons, Menger, and Walras at that time. The fundamental principle of marginalism had been implicit in the theory of population proposed by Malthus in 1798, it reappeared in explicit form in Ricardo's theory of differential rent in 1817, and it had been stated by the French economist Turgot in 1765 and by West and Torrens in England in 1815 (see Landreth and Colander 1989, 82). Further, a reasonably complete statement of the marginal productivity theory of income distribution had been made by Johann Heinrich von Thünen in 1850 in his *Der Isolierte Staat*. The theory of utility maximization had been grounded in the concept of marginal utility in Herman Heinrich Gossen's important work in 1854, *The Laws of Human Relations and the Rules of Human Action Derived Therefrom*. What came to be referred to as Gossen's first and second laws came to reexpression in the marginalist theories of the last quarter of the nineteenth century, a development that aligned also with the anticipation of the marginal utility concept in the work of Dupuit in 1844.

The classical economists' conception of demand forces in the market was sharply refocused in the 1870s by the emphasis on the subjective, self-interested evaluations placed on commodities by individuals who demanded them. The notion of such self-interested subjective evaluations had been introduced to economic argument in the medieval-scholastic period (see Dempsey [1935] 1960) and had been explicitly discussed by a number of writers before Smith's *Wealth of Nations* in 1776. In 1750 Ferdinando Galiani, in his *Della Moneta*, had argued that the ratio of exchange between two commodities, or their relative values, depended on their relative utility and scarcity (see Niehans 1990, 119). Within the classical period William Forster Lloyd had provided an explicit formulation of the concept of diminishing marginal utility in his *Lecture on the Notion of Value, as Distinguishable not only from Utility but also from Value in Exchange* in 1834.

The notion of utility, and in particular that of utility realizations at the margin, had been explicitly articulated also by Daniel Bernoulli, who published an important paper in Latin in 1738. It was translated in 1968 under the title "Exposition of a New Theory of Risk Evaluation." In that paper the concept of the diminishing marginal utility of income or wealth, but not, of course, the issue of the ethical relevance of it that will concern us in what follows, was explicitly formalized. And in due course, wider conceptions of utility entered the economics discipline from the philosophy of utilitarianism.

In the classical period the concept of utility was accorded extensive treatment by the movement referred to as philosophic radicalism, an amalgam, in many respects, of arguments from political economy and moral philosophy. The movement was associated principally with Jeremy Bentham (1748–1832) and has been accorded quasi-definitive treatment in Elie Halevy's *The Growth of Philosophic Radicalism* ([1928] 1955). In Bentham's famous moral arithmetic the interests of individuals were reckoned to be identical (Halevy, xviii), and this led to some well-known propositions regarding the maximum benefit, or utility, that might accrue to society as a whole from certain forms of action or behavior. As Lindsay observed in his preface to the Halevy volume, "The Benthamites were influenced by their belief in the possibilities of applying to the study of man and society the principles and methods of the Physical sciences," or the principles of Newton that had been introduced a century earlier.

Bentham's moral arithmetic, or the "felicific calculus," implied the existence of measurable quantities of pleasure or pain that might result from various actions or economic decisions or modes of behavior. It was thought possible to take a sum of pleasures and to set against them a sum of pains which were conceived of as negative pleasures. A proposed action was understood to be good if the balance of the calculus was on the side of pleasure rather than pain. The utilitarian assumption of the identity of interests led to the same vision of the existence of automatic or spontaneous harmonies in the economic system as it did in the case of Adam Smith (see Halevy [1928] 1955, 16–17). Further, because all individuals were to be counted equally in economic society, actions could be judged morally on the basis of the balance of their effect on aggregate human happiness. That led, as has frequently been observed, to the notion that education and legislation should be directed to promoting the greatest happiness of the greatest number, though Niehans observes that that last mentioned phrase was originated by Francis Hutcheson, the professor of moral philosophy who was Adam Smith's teacher at the University of Glasgow (Niehans 1990, 60).

In the light of these developments, the emphasis on the concept of marginal utility that gained widened currency in the 1870s was something of a rediscovery. It is true that the full and complete integration of the marginal utility apparatus into systematic economics did wait until the latter decades of the nineteenth century, and at that time it was fairly definitively incorporated into both supply and demand analysis. But the parentage of the concept is clarified by Jevons's acknowledgment, in the preface to his *Theory of Political Economy* in 1871, that he was concerned explicitly to develop the "Calculus of Pleasure and Pain" ([1871] 1957, vi). Jevons observes, in setting the frame for his argument, that "we must

undoubtedly accept what Bentham has laid down upon this subject . . ."
([1871] 1957, 28).

RECENT PHILOSOPHIC EMPHASES

Economics as a discipline gradually, or with accelerating pace in the high
days of neoclassicism, surrendered its erstwhile relations with moral philosophy. Hahn and Hollis have lamented the "oddly little commerce"
between the two disciplines, following the trends "when economics was
turning itself into a closed, technical discipline with the aid of Logical
Positivism and against the wishes of those who valued its leadership of the
moral sciences" (1979, 1).

An aspect of the utilitarianism that gained an upper hand at that time is
implicit in Gewirth's engaging lecture on "Moral Rationality" ([1972] 1976,
113–50), though Gewirth does not set out there to address the utilitarian
principle directly. He is concerned rather with the larger "question whether
a moral principle can be rationally justified," and he comments on the
"central place [of that question] in philosophical ethics" ([1972] 1976, 113;
see also, for a discussion of the rationalist grounding of ethics, Harsanyi
1982). The difficulty with which Gewirth is principally concerned is that of
establishing a rational justification for "the moral point of view."

Of principal moment for our present purposes, that philosophic question of the nature and the function or the office of rationality brings recent
discussion into contact with the economists' assumption of the autonomous
and rational economic man. Robert Nozick has recently structured his
investigation into *The Nature of Rationality* on an anthropological postulate whose implications extend to the heart of the utilitarian debate.

The capacity to be rational demarcates humans from other animals and thus
defines them. Human specialness has repeatedly been contracted since the Middle
Ages . . . Copernicus, Darwin, and Freud taught us that human beings do not
occupy a special place in the universe, they are not special in their origin and are
not always guided by rational or even consciously known motives. . . . The Greeks
saw rationality as independent of animality, certainly not its outgrowth.
*Evolutionary theory makes it possible to see rationality as one among other animal
traits, an evolutionary adaptation with a delimited purpose and function.* . . . [P]hilos-
ophy's traditional problems . . . result from attempts to extend rationality beyond
its delimited evolutionary function. (1993, xi–xii, italics added)

In this specification of the traditional philosophic problem we hear the
echo of the Kantian assumption of the autonomous individual. But a philosophic tension enters at that point. It stems from the fact that in a basic
sense utilitarianism, as we are now considering it as an ethical doctrine,
obliterates the individual person. That is so in the respect that utilitarianism regards the individual as simply, or substantially, a locus of utility. That

narrowing of the plane of explanation applies also to societal, as distinct from individual, applications. When, that is, the identification of individual utilities is extracted from specific economic situations or behavior possibilities, and when those individual utilities are summed to ascertain the balance of pleasure and pain for the larger social entity, all other considerations that identify the person are submerged and are not of analytic concern (see Sen and Williams 1982, 5). When, moreover, the criteria implicit in utilitarianism are directed to the propriety of public or social choice, the individual's personal autonomy is relatively neglected.

Gewirth, however, in the essay to which we have referred, has pointed precisely to the possibility of justifying "the principle of an egalitarian-universalist morality" ([1972] 1976, 116), and it is that principle that has clear kinship with the notions of utility and utilitarianism. The details of the argument by which Gewirth justifies such a principle rest on the supposition of "the voluntariness and purposiveness which every agent necessarily has in acting, and which he necessarily claims as rights for himself." Such rights, in turn, each agent "must also, on pain of self-contradiction, admit to be rights of [others]" ([1972] 1976, 130). For those others "are similar to him in being prospective agents who want to fulfill their purposes" ([1972] 1976, 130). It is then the statement of such rights that "constitutes an egalitarian-universalist moral principle" ([1972] 1976, 130). The principle, "Apply to your recipient [the other person acted upon by, or engaged in a "transaction" with, a purposively acting agent] the same categorical features of action that you apply to yourself," Gewirth calls the "Principle of Categorical Consistency (PCC)" ([1972] 1976, 135). "Every rational agent must accept the PCC on pain of self-contradiction" ([1972] 1976, 139).

Gewirth's position is similar to that of Harsanyi, who observes that "utilitarian ethics makes all of us members of the same moral community." For "according to utilitarian theory, the fundamental basis of all our moral commitments to other people is a general goodwill and human sympathy" (1982, 56). Here Adam Smith's *Theory of Moral Sentiments* is echoed. (A similar conception of utilitarianism that views utility in terms of desires and their fulfillment is inherent in the defense of utilitarian ethical theory made by Hare (1982, 23–38; see also Sen and Williams 1982, 11)).

To extend these lines of analysis is to recognize that utilitarianism, in one way or another, carries with it the notion of a possible extension to concepts of equality or egalitarianism. It raises the tension, that is, that we have referred to as that between individuality and solidarity. That tension impacts, moreover, on the sustainability of a doctrine of rights, such as Gewirth proposed. It impacts, that is, on the consistency between the conception of individual rights and the coherence of utilitarianism as a social doctrine. A single example will illustrate the point. An individual, it may be supposed, may be understood to acquire utility from the satisfaction of his or her wish that another person should act in a specified way. But then the question of that other person's rights comes into view. Some people's utility or degree of satisfaction may be enhanced, to take a prominent contemporary example, if other people's right to abortion were abolished. But such an abolition may infringe upon what other people, rightly or wrongly, and on whatever moral grounds are adduced, imagine to be their rights.

It may well be the case, that is, that the fulfillment of one person's wish may violate another person's individual rights or his or her prerogative of self-interested self-determination. In that case the locus of individual utilities, which might in other circumstances and in general be candidates for summation to aggregate social utilities, may not be validly conceived as aggregatable at all. The problem that is thereby posed is akin to that treated in Sen's classic paper on "The Impossibility of a Paretian Liberal" (1970, reprinted in Hahn and Hollis 1979, 127–133). The problem that arises is that of the interdependence of personal preferences and of the conflict of rights that may follow from the expression of those preferences. An instance that impinges explicitly on the economics of the market was noted earlier in connection with the tobacco industry. The assumption of an individual right to nicotine consumption may offend wider standards of cultural or scientific, and conceivably ethical, criteria.

Ethical questions thus inhere in any suggestion that in the interests of social coherence certain trade-offs of one person's rights against those of another, or trade-offs between different kinds of generalized rights, may be contemplated. But for purposes of ethical analysis, such as the question of utility that we are now addressing implies, any attempt to ground ethical criteria in a recognition of individual rights renders extremely difficult the aggregation of the rights of different people into a homogeneous totality. It is that, however, that certain expressions of universalistic utilitarianism envisage.

ECONOMIC IMPLICATIONS

Economic argument recognizes that different individuals enter the economic and market process with different wealth endowments, opportunities, preferences, and tastes. It acknowledges also that differences in abilities, talents, skills, mobilities, and degrees of ambition and motivation exist. For those reasons economics, so far as it looks to a basis of justification in moral philosophy, is more likely to be interested in and concerned about equity than it is about equality. But in one way or another, the principal implication of utilitarianism has been that the chief end of moral action should be, for the individual, his well-being. That has been interpreted as general utility in some suitably defined sense. Alternatively, the criterion has been the individual's contribution to the greatest good of society as a whole, or the greatest achievable good of the greatest possible number of the members of society.

Utilitarianism can thus be interpreted as a hedonistic philosophy. In the form stated it raises a consequentialist moral criterion. Its calculus of pleasure and pain sets out to maximize the net realization of pleasure. Although initially it was imagined that both pleasure and pain could be cardinally measured, the ordinalist revolution at the hands of Edgeworth (1881), Pareto ([1909] 1971), Hicks and Allen (1934), and Hicks ([1939] 1946) changed that. Jevons, who took over the Benthamite calculus, claimed that "the ultimate quantities which we treat in Economics are Pleasures and Pains [and] our most difficult task will be to express their dimensions correctly" (1871] 1957, 65). He then concluded quite simply that "pleasure and pain must be regarded as measured upon the same scale, and as having, therefore, the same dimensions, being quantities of the same kind, which can be added and subtracted; they differ only in sign or direction."

In its significance for market activity, utilitarianism pointed to the notions of the simple system of natural liberty and the classical conception of competitive markets and minimal state interference that Smith's *Wealth of Nations* had endorsed (see Vickers 1995). At the height of the philosophic influence of the system, at the point, perhaps, at which its influence began to wane, John Stuart Mill presented the argument for the moral worth of happiness that was taken to underlie the expression of market demands. This Mill found in the simple fact that people desire happiness.

[T]he sole evidence it is possible to produce that anything is desirable, is that people do actually desire it. . . . No reason can be given why the general happiness is desirable except that each person, so far as he believes it to be attainable, desires his own happiness. ([1861] 1957, 44, quoted in Welch 1987, 4:772)

Mill, in his *Principles*, gives a much more extended treatment to the utilities produced by different kinds and applications of labor ([1848] 1961, 45–46), and he examines the market conditions under which "Utility rushes up to its highest and ultimate gradation" (444). But to focus for the moment on Mill's statement regarding happiness that we have just noted, a significant problem is inherent in it. For from the ethical perspectives that are brought into view it leaves open the possibility that market demands may thereby be expressed for commodities, the production and consumption of which might be thought to be, on other grounds, morally reprehensible and subject to social and cultural disapprobation.

Mill's principle, however, is echoed in much of modern microeconomic and market theorizing. It appears in Harsanyi's defense of what he refers to as "preference utilitarianism," in relation to which he proposes "the important philosophic principle of *preference autonomy*." "By this I mean," Harsanyi continues in Millian terms, "the principle that, in deciding what is good and what is bad for a given individual, the ultimate criterion can only be his own wants and his own preferences" (1982, 55). Interestingly, however, Harsanyi does acknowledge a possible exceptive case.

To be sure, as I will myself argue below, a person may irrationally want something which is very 'bad for him.' But, it seems to me, the only way we can make sense of such a statement is to interpret it as a claim to the effect that, in some appropriate sense, his own preferences at some deeper level are inconsistent with what he is now trying to achieve. (1982, 55)

But a full development of such a preference-based utilitarianism is somewhat different from, or retains a tenuous logical relation to, the pleasure-pain approach that Bentham had initially introduced. In any event, the ethical dilemma inherent in the possible exceptive cases that Harsanyi has recognized is whether grounds can be adduced for the assumption that individuals can be educated to recognize their own best interest consistently and to express their desires, preferences, and choices accordingly. That dilemma raises pointedly also, of course, a further question. It has to do with who, and on what grounds and against what deeper justificatory criteria, can be mandated to formulate objectives of both individual true self-interest and the social good.

At such a point one may be understandably enticed to dogmatize on the form and formulation of the ethical criteria that should be adduced. But the arrogance of dogmatism would be misplaced. More important at such a stage is the recognition of the issues of moral import that call for address. First, moralities which, on grounds of deeper ethical sensitivities, have gained cultural acceptability may dictate the impropriety of certain lines of personal consumption behavior. Forms of vice, pornography, or drug trafficking exemplify the issue. Second, such culturally determined or acceptable principles may themselves derive from scientific advances (as in the deleterious effects of nicotine consumption and its attendant social and economic costs) or personal deontic criteria (as in the case of fetus abortion). They may be, of course, arguable or controvertible on alternative philosophic grounds.

The argument to this point has implied what has been termed egoistic utilitarianism. From whatever deeper determinative principles demand decisions emanate, they raise a further problem for the meaning of economic argument. When pleasure-providing events or outcomes or choices are introduced into the pleasure-pain calculus, those outcomes themselves stand on equal ground as to their moral evaluation. What is more, the problem arises, as Hare has acknowledged in his defense of utilitarianism, that the economic conception of "the diminishing marginal utility of all commodities and of money . . . means that approaches towards equality will tend to increase total utility." And further, "inequalities tend to produce, at any rate in educated societies, envy, hatred and malice, whose disutility needs no emphasising" (1982, 27).

The recognition of these issues, however, raises the question of the validity or the sustainability of interpersonal comparisons of utility. It was the perceived impossibility of such interpersonal comparisons that influenced Robbins's construction of his methodological *Essay* and his argument for a rigorous demarcation of economics from ethics. But if, for the moment, the notion of utility is transmuted to that of "well-being," it is significant that a revival of interest in the possibility of meaningful interpersonal comparisons has recently been canvassed. Recent analysis has argued that "a number of concepts of well-being . . . may lend themselves to interpersonal comparisons" (Elster and Roemer 1993, 5). Elster and Roemer have characterized the work in that direction by observing that

Along one dimension, they [the concepts lending themselves to interpersonal comparisons] may be divided into subjective mental states (hedonic satisfaction), degree of objective satisfaction of subjective desires, and objective states. Along another dimension, they may be differentiated through the principles by which states of pleasure or desire-satisfaction are admitted or discarded as components of well-being. (1993, 5).

But it is not universally agreed that interpersonal comparisons are legitimately possible and usable in the manner intended. The discussion surrounding Harsanyi's defense of utilitarianism (in the Sen and Williams volume, 1982, 39–62) instances the point (see Elster and Roemer 1993, 13–14). In his conclusion as to "Morality and the theory of rational behavior," in which he echoes the problem and concerns that Gewirth addressed ([1972] 1976), Harsanyi notes that

I have tried to show that an updated version of classical utilitarianism is the only ethical theory consistent with both the modern theory of rational behaviour and a full commitment to an impartially sympathetic humanitarian morality. (1982, 61).

That highly interesting debate notwithstanding, the claim can be made, as in the present argument, that all such issues and possible defenses of utilitarianism founder on the reality of the uniqueness, separability, and psychological individuality and sanctity of persons engaged in the economic and social process. For at a minimum, two further considerations stand in the way of both interpersonal comparisons of utility and the maintenance of utilitarianism as an explanatory and significant economic doctrine.

First, it is in no sense clear that individuals are able consistently to articulate an explanatory relation between their stated preferences and their deeper or so-called second-order preferences, where the latter motivate their expressed desires and are conceived to be consistent with them. Second, it follows from the ignorance thus involved that there is no reason to believe that such deeper or philosophically motivated preferences, or preferences that emanate from individual belief-systems, can carry over into assumed social aggregates when a plurality of such belief-systems exist. Individual utilities will not in any case, that is, be aggregatable.

On the level of market analysis, individuals do not enter the demand side of the market with clearly stated and stable preferences. Contrary to the neoclassical postulate of autonomous and exogenous market partici-pants, individuals are formed, as to their epistemic status and economic characteristics, by their participation in the market process itself (see Hollis and Nell, 1975, 183). But it is clear also that notwithstanding the log-ical difficulties inherent in attempts at interpersonal comparisons, such comparisons are frequently implicit in economists' policy recommenda-tions. In matters of fiscal policy, progressive tax rates, welfare payments, and income redistributions, such assumptions are made, rightly or wrongly, on the level of empirical realities.

At such a point also, the same damaging reality that impacts on all attempts at aggregation in economic analysis is relevant. The logical prob-lems involved in the specification of the simple and widely employed con-sumer demand curve may serve as an example. At a minimum, the individual consumer's statement as to the amounts of a commodity he or she may purchase at differently stated prices provides at best a notional demand curve that is based on a number of crucial assumptions. These include the assumption that in the event of the availability of the com-modity at a stated price, all of the individual's purchase or sale intentions in all other markets will be able to be consummated at the prices and the quantity levels initially envisaged. Those other prices may include the prices at which certain commodity endowments or endowments of labor time and employable skills will be able to be marketed. Those assumed market prices, in turn, influence the level of the initial endowment upon which the original notional purchase intention is based. Or, alternatively, the initial value endowment may incorporate the present discounted value of future expected income streams that asset endowments might generate. In that case there does not exist any necessary guarantee that when, as was supposed, the commodity whose purchase is in view actually becomes available, the endowment value on which the original notional purchase intention was stated will then be as initially supposed.

All of these considerations and others related to them, (such as, at a minimum, the individual's inability to know what unexpected market opportunities might be available when commodity offers at designated prices are actually made), mean that statements of notional purchase intentions are made against what we may now refer to as individuals' severely stated or imagined ceteris paribus assumptions. But further, dif-ferent market participants will undoubtedly come to the market with quite differently conceived ceteris paribus assumptions. There is then no logical coherence in the argument that separate individuals' purchase intentions, understood now as notional intentions in the sense stated, can be summed to specify a market demand curve, when, as is now argued, the assumed content of the ceteris paribus is different for different individuals. The same problem of the incompatibility of different individuals' ceteris paribus assumptions, or of what lies behind their stated conceptions of possible utility realizations, renders problematic the aggregation that univeralistic utilitarianism contemplates (see Vickers 1995, 111ff.).

A SUGGESTED SOLUTION

Utilitarianism has been transmuted in various ways into economic analysis. The initial psychological theory that informed Bentham's proposals, and that led Jevons to contemplate a measurable utility scale that would calibrate pleasure and pain in comparable units, was in due course replaced by the theory of preference orderings and ordinal utility functions (see Shackle 1967, chaps. 7 and 8). The concepts of measurability or calibration did, however, continue to attract the attention of some of the profoundest thinkers in the economics discipline (see Fisher 1927; Mirrlees 1982; Samuelson's "Note on the Measurement of Utility" 1937). On that point Mirrlees reaches the conclusion that

In a society of isomorphic individuals, i.e. individuals who are the same with respect to some way of comparing their experiences, the outcomes of economic (or social) policies ought to be evaluated by adding their individual utilities, because everyone ought to agree to have every other individual treated as one of his alternative selves. (1982, 83)

Mirrlees's position here recalls the "Principle of Categorical Consistency" that Gewirth enunciated earlier. Mirrlees goes on to give such a conclusion moral import. But the notion he employs of isomorphism is a theoretic construction that projects only tenuous analogies to the economic world. The real and acute problem that confronts the economist is that of contemplating acceptable ethical criteria, both as to individual behavior and aggregative social policies, in conditions of markedly distinct and differentiated individuals. That problem has been implied in Hahn's rejoinder to Mirrlees. The "cardinalisation" that Mirrlees has just envisaged

cannot be derived from the preferences of agents over social states unless the agents are essentially alike and also utilitarians. . . . Hence different utilitarians with different cardinalisations can come to different policy conclusions. The disagreement between them will turn on their social preferences and it is not clear that it is resolvable. (Hahn 1982, 187)

And of course, as Hahn observes, not all reasonable and serious persons may be utilitarians. Some, following Rawls, for example, may rank, say, liberty ahead of utility (Hahn 1982, 187–88).

The introduction of the utility concept to the theory of "games and economic behavior" (von Neumann and Morgenstern [1944] 1947; Luce and Raiffa 1957, chap. 2; Vickrey 1945), which again involved a quasi-cardinalization, recalled the notion of betting rates as an approach to the calibration of subjective probabilities that de Finetti had earlier introduced ([1937] 1964; see also Vickers 1994). In doing so it integrated with risk analysis a hybrid cardinal-ordinal notion of utility. (Relevant issues are addressed in Tobin 1958, Arrow 1971, Diamond and Rothschild 1978, and Georgescu-Roegen 1966.) But in due course the ordinality of, for example, Edgeworth (1881), Pareto ([1909] 1971), Hicks and Allen (1934), and Hicks ([1939] 1946) came to be regarded as canonical. Economic analysis at that point has taken preference orderings, as defined, for example, over commodity bundles, as prespecified and generally as intertemporally stable. It has then proceeded to examine the implications for individual choice and for market valuations of optimizing behavior that might logically be derived from such preference relations.

But a number of problems inhere in that standard analysis. In the first place, as Hahn's example of the work week suggests, one might realize utility maximization by working eight hours a day for five days a week as a result of a free and uninhibited decision. But if, say, a government law were passed that compulsorily required work for eight hours a day for five days a week, the individual might feel worse off by reason of the constraint and the loss of liberty that the new law imposed (Hahn 1982, 188). Again, the level of one's individual utility may depend on the level and distribution of the aggregate social income in which he or she shares. In Mill's conception of the stationary state, for example,

there would be as much scope as ever [in that halcyon state] for all kinds of mental culture, and moral and social progress; as much room for improving the Art of Living, and much more likelihood of its being improved, when minds ceased to be engrossed by the art of getting on. ([1848] 1961, 751)

Or as in Duesenberry's theory of consumption, the utility that individuals derive from consumption expenditures may depend on where they stand in the distribution of income relative to the rest of the population. Their utility then depends on some notion of the population average consumption expenditures, or, in another interpretation, on the consumption possibilities of the socio-economic class with which they identify (Duesenberry 1949).

A PRELIMINARY EVALUATION

For our present purposes, the point of interest that emerges from an evaluation of utilitarianism is that of the ethical import or the moral significance of the criteria that are derived from it. That it is in general consequentialist and hedonistic has been adequately observed. The morality of actions or policies or outcomes is determined, in the utilitarian system of thought, by the goodness or utility or net pleasure that is derived or generated. In that sense it sets up a clear, or at least a logically well-defined, ethical calculus. From the evaluative perspective held at present, its criteria are not clearly deontologically defined.

Moreover, the levels of utility attained by different individuals will not necessarily be measurable. But in spite of that fact, the system has nevertheless been imagined to lead to certain admissible schemes of economic distribution and distributive justice. When those issues are addressed, the utilitarian ethical calculus has been assumed to be applicable to a number of related policy problems. A reliance on the economists' notion of the diminishing marginal utility of income, for example, has pointed, in terms of the utilitarian ethical calculus, to the maximization of aggregate welfare by redistributions toward income equality (see Rothschild 1993, 124ff.). That itself, it will be seen in the next chapter, raises issues of acute ethical import and opens scope for ethically acceptable systems of income, wealth, and welfare distribution.

The important question of income distribution is relevant to our present concern with individuals' market demands for at least two reasons. First, ethical criteria attach to the provision of an income for each individual that permits expression of market demand at a level that is minimally acceptable or ethically tolerable. That issue points clearly to that of economic or distributive justice. Second, the distribution of income that exists at any time thus influences individuals' conceptions of attainable levels of satisfaction or utility. It may generate, that is to say, feelings of socio-cultural identification, or envy, or new degrees of aspiration and motivation.

TECHNICAL ANALYSIS AND ETHICAL IMPORT

An extensive technical analysis of individual and market demand lies beyond our present objectives. The construction of that analysis on the basis of generally accepted assumptions and procedures is readily available in the standard literature (see Katzner 1988). But one significant aspect of individual demand, that of the widely held notion of marginal utility, or in particular diminishing marginal utility, raises ethical considerations. Analysis on that level invokes the notions of egoistic utilitarianism or egoistic hedonism.

The argument that Marshall established for the generation of an individual's commodity demand curve from his marginal utility curve is well known. Marshall's assumption of the constancy of the marginal utility of money for the individual (Marshall 1920, 95) permitted the transformation of the utility relation into the commodity demand relation. That assumption is to be compared, however, with Marshall's supposition for other analytical purposes that "the marginal utility of money is greater for the poor than the rich" (1920, 95). As cardinal utility gave way to ordinality and to the introduction of indifference curve analysis, the notion of marginal utility fell into something of disrepute. At least it was acknowledged that the marginal utility as derived from an ordinal utility function, one that was unique up to a monotonic positive transformation, did not possess the same interpretative significance or mathematically manipulable properties as that concept had been accorded in the context of cardinality. But significance was nevertheless attached to the ratio between marginal utilities, or between the partial derivatives of an ordinal utility function with respect to different arguments, say commodities. That ratio, where, of course, the utilities generated by different commodities were measured on the same ordinal scale, was christened the rate of substitution between the commodities. In familiar ways, variations in the optimally attainable rate of substitution in response to changes of commodity prices again permitted the logical derivation of individual commodity demand curves.

In one way or another, then, the question arises whether considerations of ethical criteria are adequately satisfied by the optimization of individual utilities, in the sense implicit in such theories of expenditure and commodity choice. For although in the more modern expression of the theory the notion of measurable utility has been replaced by the ranking of preferences, the underlying notions of the Benthamite utilitarian calculus remain inherent in the analysis. Two considerations would appear to bear on the answer to the question; first, whether an individual's subjective evaluation of his or her prospective utility satisfaction is reliable in the sense that ethical propriety can be attached to the results of the choices and actions that emanate from it; and second, whether, at the level of universalization, individual choices do in fact point to the desired or maximally achievable level of common good.

The first of these questions is not intended to be as radical as might appear. Consider, in that connection, a distinction within the range of concepts that utilitarianism implies. Harrod (1936) has referred to what has been labeled *act utilitarianism*. That concept refers to the proposition that the rightness of an action is judged scrupulously by the consequences of the act. Such a procedure assumes that a reliance may be placed on the soundness and admissibility of individual evaluations and judgments. But moral content may very well enter into the choice possibilities, thereby rendering inappropriate a sole reliance on contemplated consequences or outcomes.

In order to achieve consequences that are judged to be good and desirable when considered in themselves, it might be necessary to perform actions or to make choices that are morally reprehensible and unacceptable. Welch has quoted the example proposed by Godwin that if one were confronted with the "choice between saving one's mother from a burning building or saving a great man whose works were more likely to benefit mankind, one ought to save the great man" (Welch 1987, 4:774). Against such a scheme of act utilitarianism, the alternative of *rule utilitarianism* has been proposed. That procedure asks whether an action would have calculably good consequences if it were to obey a rule that was acceptable as a general practice in society.

Entering the scheme of things, that is, is the notion of the universalizability of ethical rules in the manner we encountered earlier. In that respect, rule utilitarianism recaptures the spirit of, for example, the Kantian categorical imperative, and it introduces a deontic element, along with utilitarian consequentialism, into ethical criteria. It projects, that is, a mixed deontological-consequentialist ethical criterion.

The relevance of these arguments to the question of market demand can be envisaged, however, without such dramatic examples as that of Godwin's burning building. The question of the reliability of individual judgment and assessment raises the possibility again that certain expressions of market demand may in themselves contain actions that are either morally or legally condemnable on grounds other than those of the utility envisaged. Or the grounds on which action is based may not in themselves imply a reasonable possibility of leading to the ends desired. What that amounts to is the possibility that ethical desiderata will not be properly served, in either the personal-egoistic or the universalistic sense, by assuming that a free-for-all and uninhibited market activity will necessarily achieve the objectives of morality that might be contemplated. The introduction to Keynes's essay on *The End of Laissez-faire* that we quoted previously is recalled. "Nor is it true," Keynes observes, "that self-interest generally is enlightened; more often individuals acting separately to promote their own ends are too ignorant or too weak to achieve even these" ([1931] 1972, 9:287–88). It is difficult to conclude, it is here implied, that ethical desiderata are necessarily satisfied in an economic and market system characterized by an extreme and uninhibited libertarianism.

It may appear on the surface to be benevolent and nonintrusive, and therefore morally proper or desirable, to allow individuals to have what they want, to the extent, that is, that those wants are expressed in market demands. But as is implied in the preceding argument, those wants might not be either rationally conceived or in the individuals' best interests. For as has been observed in other contexts, it is a demonstrable weakness of the neoclassical economic analysis to assume that individuals come to the market with preestablished, well-defined, exogenous, and unalterable tastes, resources, preferences, and aspirations. On the contrary, it is implicit in previous arguments that in the respects that have just been stated, individual market participants are constituted to a significant degree by the market process itself. It is true that individuals make markets. But it is also true that markets make individuals, at least in the relevant economic and epistemological sense.

Given, in other words, the fact that market activity takes place in real, historic time, individual market participants make their decisions and choices in the conditions of ignorance that the unidirectional arrow of time implies. Under those conditions only questionable reliance can be placed on the statement of one's initial and notional purchase intentions. Individuals, in short, do not necessarily possess adequate information to enable them to decide consistently in their own best interests. At that point, therefore, the large and ethically significant question of the provision of information arises. As was observed in the preceding chapter, the ethics of advertising and product promotion then become relevant. Product promotion, and its relation, tenuous or otherwise, to what has been labeled truth in advertising, partially determines the ethical sustainability of everywhere uninhibited market activity. It would not be difficult to cite instances of attempts to deceive and confuse, rather than to inform, or to instance cases in which manufacturers have been required by government regulations to desist from previously stated but spurious commodity claims.

What is in view at this point is not necessarily a paternalistic government intervention in the market process or in the provision of output for personal consumption demands. Involved, on the contrary, are simply three issues that may be seen, in the light of preceding discussion, to contain ethical import. First, concern properly exists, as has just been argued, for the provision of information and for truth and integrity in production and marketing. Second, as was explored in an earlier context, instances may arise in which certain uses of property may be constrained in the interests of wider social good. As a case in point, constraints may be placed on industrial freedom to pollute the environment, raising the important questions of possible forms of compensation to property owners who are disadvantaged by such pollution, and the allocation of the costs of controlling such environmental spoliation. Or constraints on, say, tobacco consumption may be thought to be desirable in the interests of wider social welfare. Third, the economics of fiscal policy, and of forms of income and wealth redistribution that will be addressed at length in the following chapter, imply again constraints on what would otherwise be uninhibited individual consumption. At that level again it will be possible to contemplate ethical criteria.

The issues that have just been raised contemplate the rightness or the justifiability of official regulation of industrial claims regarding the nature and effectiveness of marketed commodities. Dilemmas for public policy arise quickly and acutely in that respect. To take again a previously cited case as a single example, the dilemma was recently faced as to whether nicotine should or should not be declared an addictive drug and its product use brought under more intensive government regulation. The arguments for and against commodity prohibition, which, of course, had been adopted at an earlier time in the United States in connection with alcohol consumption, are well canvassed. But ethical acuteness might be thought to arise in the case of nicotine in the light of scientific testimony that cigarette manufacturers had earlier suppressed findings of the addictive and carcinogenic properties of nicotine.

But in any event, the availability and reliability of information would appear to influence the degree of reliance that can be placed on the actual expression of market demands as determining ethical propriety. It is not simply the case, as Simon (1972), for example, has proposed, that economic decisions, including, in the present case, consumers' decisions, are made in the context of what he referred to as bounded rationality. Rationality is bounded for Simon (1972) in the sense that too much information exists to be handled completely and efficiently. Beyond that reality lies a twofold and deeper problem.

In the first place, as one makes decisions that on the level of consumption expenditures have implications for future conditions, the actual outcomes that the future will contain are not only unknown; they are unknowable. From that it follows that the future does not exist in an external and objective ontological sense waiting to be discovered. Rather, economic choices and decisions create their own history and their own future. It is then the history-creating significance of economic choice that comes pointedly to relevance for the consideration of ethical judgment. But what that amounts to again is that it cannot be assumed that individual choices necessarily are, or that they will turn out to be, in the individual's own best interests. That remains the case, even though it might be rejoined that in the conditions of ignorance that the passing of real historical time involves one might be accorded the prerogative of judging what is thought to be in his or her own best interests. At issue also again is the necessity of the provision, in an honest and ethically justifiable sense, of as full as possible an array of relevant information.

In conditions of ignorance such as are here envisaged, reliance may be placed on certain more or less well-established economic and social conventions as guides to action. On the level of economic decisions, much was made of the relevance and implications of conventions by Keynes in his *General Theory* (1936, 152–53) and in his 1937 essay (see also Vickers 1995, 226). But in the unfolding of real economic time, the foundations of established conventions may turn out to be, as Keynes put it, flimsy. Conventions may change, even abruptly and alarmingly, when something new comes into the picture. It follows, therefore, that even if behavior in accordance with given conventions is taken to provide justifiable criteria, the need remains to examine in their own right the ethical criteria that adjudicate the morality of whatever conventions exist.

Furthermore if, in ways such as those suggested, ethical desiderata are not necessarily served by uninhibited market choice and activity, then it is the more difficult to conceive that ethical criteria ensue from the aggregation of individual desires or preferences, such as classic utilitarianism supposed. For if, as has been clarified from more than one perspective, individuals can be misguided in the matter of what has been labeled the content of the ceteris paribus assumptions in terms of which their decisions are made, then a previous logical problem is again confronted. That is the problem of aggregating in any meaningful sense the desires, preferences, and intentions of individuals whose ceteris paribus assumptions are differently defined, inconsistent, and irreconcilable.

On the level of market analysis, further, the question of the ethical appropriateness of certain kinds of commodity demands, consumption, and production is again relevant. Relevant also is the previously noted distinction that Sen has made between a narrowly defined self-interest and such determinants as commitment and sympathy. What is involved in such considerations is that a stringent and narrow egoistic utilitarianism again falls short of exclusive ethical propriety. Of course a utility function can conceivably be defined over any number of arguments, not all of which are necessarily quantifiable, to include acknowledgments of desirable objectives other than self-interest. Or it might be conceived that one's self-interest is in fact served by the expression of sympathy and commitment. It is the recognition of such possibilities that, as remarked in our earlier discussion of meta-ethical vocabulary, blurs the distinction between deontological and teleological or consequentialist criteria.

But a sense of the deontic or the obligatory may enter the market demand decision at several further points. First, ethical propriety is arguably relevant to the basic decision regarding the allocation of income or resources to either consumption or saving. The economists' analytical apparatus of time preference, or what the Austrian economists termed telescopic foresight, or the individual's ability or willingness to make provision for his or her personal future, instances the point. Moral responsibility exists at that point for the provision within the economic and social framework of an institutional structure that facilitates and motivates individual saving. That provision influences not only individual welfare, but also the possible flow of investable funds in the money capital markets, the effective costs of industrial capital, industrial capital formation, and the attainable rates of growth in the economy at large. For the encouragement and facilitation of personal saving, certain familiar income tax incentives will therefore be relevant and their ethical justification accordingly established.

Second, it is arguable that ethical desiderata attach in further respects to the form and structure of market demand. Conspicuous consumption, for example, might ethically be called in question in certain economic conjunctures. The point at issue touches the question of the rightness or otherwise, on morally justifiable grounds, of the allocation to consumption of economic resources that, against aggregative criteria, might be allocated to the alleviation of basic needs at identifiable points of society. Galbraith's *The Affluent Society* (1958) has addressed the issue. For our present purposes only a twofold relevance might be noted.

In the first place, a universalistic as against the previous egoistic ethic is thereby brought into view. At issue is the good, in some arguable sense, of the social entity as a whole. In some respects it might appear that emphasis thereby shifts from what was previously referred to as act utilitarianism to rule utilitarianism. Certainly the question arises as to whether a rule or rules can be contemplated that will guide effectively, from whatever ethical as well as economically efficient criteria might be proposed, different individuals' decisions and actions.

Secondly, the issue of acceptable morality arises in the distribution of the economy's resources between the satisfaction of private sector and public sector demands. The question of the proper role of the government and the degree of its intrusion into market activity is, of course, open to ideological and philosophic argument on levels that do not address primarily the issue of ethical desiderata. The case for what has frequently been referred to as the mixed economy, resting on grounds of political as well as economic philosophy, does not need to detain us in the present context. The observation has already been made that difficulty inheres in the acceptance on ethical grounds of a completely uninhibited laissez faire or libertarian market system. Too many people, through no fault of their own, can be thrown aside and left in less than morally acceptable condition by the uninhibited march of libertarian markets.

Reasons exist also why, quite apart from issues of income and resource sharing and the distributions of economic benefit that are involved, sensible provision at the public sector level needs to be made for the erection and preservation of an economically viable infrastructure. The question of ethical criteria enters that arena in a number of respects. First, it does not need to be emphasized that morality attaches to the responsibility for the efficient employment of public sector resources. The recent cases in the United States of defense industry contractors submitting fictitious invoices and charges to government purchasers, the apparent overcharging, and the exploitation of cost-plus pricing contracts are available for inspection.

Second, at the institutional level, understanding that certain institutional practices and prerogatives may derive from governmental regulations or deregulation, ethical conduct that satisfies desiderata of integrity and social responsibility is clearly mandated. The establishment of institutional structures, which may arise not only from freely functioning market activity and preferences but also from the conduct of centralized policy in the interest of aggregative social welfare, opens the door to a variety of legal constraints and regulations. In that matter an entry to ethical criteria is provided, first at the level of the objectives and purposes in view in the establishment of institutions, and second at the level of the functioning of them and the exploitation or otherwise of opportunities for private advantage they may make possible. On the first level the end in view may well contain aspects of morality in relation, for example, to the provision of minimal economic welfare for otherwise disadvantaged citizens. On the second level opportunities for exploitation and personal gain may result from, for example, security market trading and the use for that purpose of insider information.

CONCLUDING COMMENT

It follows from the foregoing that against the assumptions of either classic egoistic or universalistic utilitarianism it is difficult to conclude on grounds of ethical criteria, whether act or rule utilitarianism is in view, that freely expressed market demands can necessarily be taken to provide morally acceptable results. The difficulty that is involved may be abated, of course, by any amount of philosophical or ideological argument or presupposition. But what is at issue is the basic fact, as it is here seen, that in any event the need exists for an ethical evaluation of market actions, demands, decisions, and choices. That is so from the perspectives of the ends in view in market action, on the demand side as well as the supply side, and from the viewpoint of the integrity of conduct that is involved.

The relevant ethical desiderata may not be adequately served simply by a narrowly defined self-interest. Address to the Adam Smith of the *Theory of Moral Sentiments* may be as seriously required as that to the Smith of the *Wealth of Nations*. Or perhaps, if the intellectual history of our subject is to be rightly understood, the moral sentiments that lived a subterranean life in the *Wealth of Nations* need to be carefully and more influentially surfaced. More difficult levels of argumentation arise in market economics than simply the severe a prioristic deductivism that Ricardo bequeathed and that the canonical neoclassicism and its "rational economic man" purveyed.

7 ETHICS AND ECONOMIC DISTRIBUTION

Issues of moral import bear heavily on the distribution of income, wealth, and welfare in the economy. For the extent to which individuals share in the benefits of the economic process depends vitally on the distribution of endowments with which they enter, or have the opportunity to enter and participate in, the economy's productive and market activity. At the same time, and given for the moment the distribution of initial endowments, questions of morality attach to the distribution of the results of the national production that are realized by, or become the shares of, different individuals or social and economic classes.

Our objective in this chapter is to explore a number of issues that emanate from those basic propositions. We will take up questions of both technical economic argument and ethical criteria.

THE STRUCTURE OF THE ARGUMENT

The discussion that follows will incorporate three levels of argument: first, some minimal aspects of more technical economic analysis; second, the relevance of certain assumptions of ethical criteria that have been raised in the preceding chapters; and third, certain recommendations regarding desirable or ethically acceptable forms of income and benefit distribution.

Technical Analysis

A number of concepts that have become embedded in technical discussion will be explored briefly in order to bring into focus the moralities and the ethical concerns they involve. They are related to Pareto optimality and welfare economics. In relation to both those areas, the following argument will present only the main outlines of the relevant analyses.

Pareto optimality, it was seen, has to be understood as not distribution-free. By that it is meant that where participants end up in a market trading process depends on the distribution of endowments with which they begin. In technical terms, the point on the Edgeworthian contract curve at which a Pareto-optimal distribution of trading outcomes occurs will depend on that initial endowment distribution. Each such initial starting point will lead to a different Pareto-optimal trading result. It is therefore pointless to dismiss the Pareto-optimality arguments as having to do simply with questions of economic efficiency. An important morality content is also involved. It concerns the ethical acceptability or otherwise of the basic resource and endowments distributions that exist.

Technical welfare economics, it will be seen, proceeded through at least two significant phases before it ran into something of an intellectual dead end. An older welfare economics stemmed from Pigou's famous work and invoked with greater or lesser consistency the notion of the diminishing marginal utility of income or wealth. Proposals for income redistribution were accordingly based upon it.

More modern welfare arguments, worried by the difficulties of such implied interpersonal comparisons of utility, centered their analysis on a set of so-called compensation principles. The question was asked whether, following a redistribution of resources, the achievable level of benefits would enable the gainers to compensate the losers in such a way as to lead to an improved overall social condition. The outlines of arguments attributable to Kaldor, Hicks, Bergson, and Scitovsky will illustrate the point.

Ethical Criteria

It is at the point of the distribution of economic benefits that a tension we noted at the beginning comes most forcibly to expression. That is the tension in the formation of ethical criteria between individuality and solidarity. We have referred, in other terms, to the tension between accountability and solidarity, or between narrowly defined economic objectives and an awareness of wider concerns and responsibilities. Now in approaching the ethics and economics of income distribution the significance of the deontic ethic of obligation enters in unique respects. For at that point there enters a sense of obligation to provide entitlements for those who are disadvantaged by the functioning, or the malfunctioning, of the economic process.

The relevance of such pressures of solidarity implies also two further levels of argument that were envisaged at the beginning. In the first place, the relevant concerns spill over to what will be referred to in the next chapter as macromorality. Obligations that are interpretable in terms of their accordance with moral sensibilities exist, that is, at the level of the conduct of macroeconomic policy and the formation of related economic institutions. Ethical responsibility devolves on those in positions of policy determination to have reason to believe that the policies instituted are pointed to ends that are ethically supportable, and that they will lead to morally satisfactory results.

Second, it has been indicated that a further concept, that of iteration, enters ethical discussion on the levels with which we are concerned at this stage. That concept enters by reason of the fact that economic activity takes place in real economic time. Consider the possibility, for example, that credence is given to the need to effect a redistribution of either income or initial endowments among individual members of the economy. As the economic and market system develops over time it will move through a future that is ever emerging and disclosing its hitherto unknown and unknowable history. As the economy develops and time unfolds, it can be reasonably anticipated that whatever distributions of welfare, benefits, income, wealth, and endowments once existed will be changed. Economic effort, outcomes, and entitlements change. The need will therefore recur to examine iteratively the situations that exist and the distributions of benefits and welfare they imply. The possibility will recur, against relevant ethical criteria, of effecting those changes that are judged to be desirable.

Redistribution Proposals

A number of proposals have recently been made for redistributions of income that are aimed to satisfy explicitly stated ethical criteria. Among those to be mentioned, prominence will be given to that of Rawls, whose *Theory of Justice* has attracted extensive comment and reaction in both the philosophic and the economic literature. At the same time, an alternative proposal will be made and some implications for aggregative economic policy will be explored.

THE REDISTRIBUTION ASSUMPTIONS

Distribution, as it is here contemplated, has to do with at least three questions: first, the distribution among members of society of endowments of economic resources; second, the processes by which, and the institutional structures through which, such given endowments or economic starting points lead to relative shares of the income generated by the economy; and third, the distribution among economic classes and among geographical and social strata of the results of the economic and market process. Individual benefits, economic institutions, and identifiable economic classes are involved.

The notion of distribution is raised in the foregoing terms in order to permit ethical attitudes to be brought to bear upon it in a corresponding threefold sense. First, it might be thought that a lack of equity exists in, or that a dissent on grounds of ethical criteria can be entered against, an existing structure of endowment distributions. Second, it might be judged on comparable grounds that inequities exist in the structure of economic processes that lead to observable results, and alterations might be called for in patterns of resource use. These might include the elimination of existing forms of discrimination and alterations in economic opportunities. Third, the results of market activity might be open to redistributions and to relevant policy measures, in the interest of satisfying ethical desiderata.

It is being argued, in other terms, that the processes of economic production and those of benefit distribution are interdependent. Proposals in that direction recall Varian's analysis of what, following the argument of Nozick, he refers to as "historical principles" and "end-state principles" of distribution (Varian [1974–75] 1979, 137; see also Nozick 1974, 50, 56). Varian there observes on Nozick's criticism of Rawls's theory that it fails to take account of the interaction of production and distribution (Varian [1974–75] 1979, 138; see also Rawls 1971).

Confronting us again at this point is the ethical robustness of the familiar "rational economic man." Johansen has pointed to the pervasive and assumedly defective assumption of the neoclassical theory at that point.

Economic theory . . . tends to suggest that people are honest only to the extent that they have economic incentives for being so. This is a homo economicus assumption which is far from being obviously true, and which needs confrontation with observed realities. In fact, a simple line of thought suggests that the assumption can hardly be true in its most extreme form. *No society would be viable without some norms and rules of conduct.* Such norms and rules are necessary for viability exactly in fields where strictly economic incentives are absent and cannot be created. (1976, quoted in Sen [1976–77] 1979, 99, italics added)

However that may be, the argument that Sen has advanced, to the effect that considerations of commitment and sympathy supplement in practice the assumedly hegemonic claims of narrow self-interest, undoubtedly makes firmer contact with economic reality. It is as though Adam Smith, in the claims he made for sympathy and fellow-feeling in his *Theory of Moral Sentiments*, argued against the clear and pronounced assumptions of self-interest in the *Wealth of Nations*.

The conventional neoclassical assumption of a narrowly-defined self-interest, then, does not appear sufficiently robust to accommodate the economic ethic we are now investigating. We are not at this point advancing an ethical principle in the manner in which, for example, Gewirth earlier defined his "Principle of Categorical Consistency (PCC)" ([1972] 1976,

135; see also chapter 6 above). At this stage our interest is not in a dogmatic proposition or a moral philosophic doctrine, but in a framework or a frame of reference within which ethical criteria and relevant economic arguments can be advanced.

WELFARE ECONOMICS BRIEFLY EXAMINED

To the extent that economic analysis has addressed the morality of distributive phenomena, its focus has been principally on the end results of the economic process. It is at that point that the subject of welfare economics has developed. Pigou's justly famous work established what became known as the Old Welfare Economics ([1932] 1962), and the New Welfare Economics of Kaldor (1939), Hicks (1939), and Bergson ([1938] 1969) has been widely discussed in the literature (see Graaf 1957, Little 1950, Sen 1982).

It should be noted, however, that in a very real sense the explicitly ethical content of the principal contributions to welfare economics has been subdued. Welfare has generally been understood as concerned, for the main part, with the acceptability of the distribution among the members of society of what the economy produces. But on another and related level, the previously mentioned analytics of Pareto-optimal trading points has absorbed economists' concern. The question has been asked whether, in a given situation, any improvement in individuals' positions could be effected by a continuation of trading exchanges. A mutually optimum position, as between trading individuals, was understood to have been reached if, as posited by the Pareto-optimum conditions, it was at that point impossible to effect a further redistribution of outcomes that would make one individual better off without at the same time making another individual worse off. At that point the trading individuals were located on the Edgeworth contract curve that is itself a locus of Pareto-optimum points.

But the explicit moral content of the argument has been unclear. Hausman and McPherson do not necessarily carry conviction in their insistence that "welfare economics rests on strong and contestable moral propositions" (1993, 673). It is no doubt true, as Hurley has argued, that values, which conceivably have moral content, inevitably constrain the descriptions of objects of preference. Hausman and McPherson, in referencing Hurley's argument, observe that "a delicious piece of apple pie that was known to be stolen would not be the same object as a physically similar piece of pie that came as a gift" (1993, 686). In some such sense, no doubt, "moral evaluations of economic arrangements are built into welfare economics" (Hausman and McPherson 1993, 689).

On the other hand, Archibald has advanced his "apparently heretical view that welfare economics does not depend upon a foundation of value judgments" (1959, 316). Holding rigorously to "the classical Robbinsian

distinction between positive and normative economics," Archibald holds
that once the ends in view are given, or once, that is, the normative issue
has been addressed if not settled, "the theorems of welfare economics are
thus theorems in positive economics" (1959, 320). "All the value judgments," Archibald observes, "come when the crucial step to prescription is
taken" (1959, 327). The methodological issue that is thereby raised is clarified further by Myint in his *Theories of Welfare Economics*. He argues that
in welfare economics "we take the wants of the individuals to be *given* and
constant and confine our study to the purely mechanical efficiency of the
economic system in satisfying these given wants" (1948, quoted in
Archibald 1959, 317).

The so-called Old Welfare Economics that did address the redistribution question was substantially utilitarian in its basic assumptions. It
assumed that sustainable conclusions as to generalized welfare could be
deduced from statements about individuals' utility realizations. It was
understood that no precise method existed to permit comparisons of the
utility levels of different persons. But notwithstanding the logical and practical inadmissibility of such interpersonal comparisons, it was nevertheless
supposed that legitimacy attached to the transfer of income from the rich
to the poor. That conclusion was based on fairly general assumptions
regarding a "law" of diminishing marginal utility. For all individuals generally, marginal utility was thought to diminish as the possession of wealth, in
the form of either goods or money, increased. While interpersonal comparisons between individuals might be inadmissible, it was thought that
between aggregated groups, or between different income and wealth
classes, significant differences existed. Differences of utility realization
existed, *on the average*, between the rich and the poor. It was then on that
ground that arguments in support of income redistribution were based. On
that point Pigou had been quite explicit.

A larger proportion of the satisfaction yielded by the incomes of rich people comes
from their *relative*, rather than their absolute, amount. This part of it will not be
destroyed if the incomes of all rich people are diminished together. The loss of economic welfare suffered by the rich when command over resources is transferred
from them to the poor will, therefore, be substantially smaller relatively to the gain
of economic welfare to the poor than a consideration of the law of diminishing utility taken by itself suggests. ([1932] 1962, 90)

Again,

It is evident that any transference of income from a relatively rich to a relatively
poor man of similar temperament, since it enables more intense wants to be satisfied at the expense of less intense wants, must increase the aggregate sum of satisfaction. The old "law of diminishing utility" thus leads securely to the proposition:
Any cause which increases the absolute share of real income in the hands of the

poor, provided that it does not lead to a contraction in the size of the national dividend from any point of view, will, in general, increase economic welfare. ([1932] 1962, 89; see also idem. Part IV chaps. 8–10)

Lying behind such propositions of the earlier welfare economics was, no doubt, the notion that morality attached, in some sense, to such redistributive claims. But the level on which morality existed was embedded in the arguments for utilitarianism that we have already addressed and which do not call for further comment at this point.

The newer welfare economics, recognizing as it did the strength of the arguments against interpersonal comparisons of utility, was markedly individualistic in its construction. In this it aligned with the methodological individualism that informed the newer subjectivist theories of the neoclassical period. In recognizing also the replacement of cardinal utility by ordinal utility that emanated from the theory of preference orderings, the new welfare economics tended to avoid speaking of total utility. Its analytical focus was on the notion of the acceptable rate of substitution between commodities or commodity bundles or the purchasing power that made the acquisition of commodities possible. The work of Kaldor and Hicks referred to above was reinforced by Scitovsky (1941), who will be seen to have offered a refinement to the Kaldor compensation principle.

The compensation principle had by that time become a central proposition of welfare economics (see Rothschild 1993, chap. 6). Its formulation followed from the concept of the Pareto-optimum trading outcome that has already been defined. The linkage of the Pareto-optimum concept with those bodies of theory can be summarized in what have become referred to as the two fundamental theorems of welfare economics. Assuming a well-defined condition of everywhere perfect competition, the welfare theorems may be stated briefly as follows.

First: The outcome of the market mechanism, or the market equilibrium, will, under very general assumptions, be a Pareto-efficient allocation.

Second: Under appropriately restrictive assumptions, it can be shown that every Pareto-efficient allocation is a market equilibrium for some initial endowment of goods. (see Varian [1974–75] 1979, 141; Bergson [1938] 1969; Lerner 1946; Arrow and Hahn 1971)

It is clear again, though the results of the theory are here severely summarized, that any statement about Pareto-efficient conditions is dependent on the initial distribution of endowments with which trading activity and participation in the economic process begins.

The newer welfare theory, moreover, is based on the proposition that the results that might be assumed to be subject to redistributive adjustment are reached as the outcome of perfectly competitive market clearing. What is at issue is the possibility of achieving, on such grounds of ethical or moral justification as might be adduced, an optimum or most desirable, feasible, or attainable outcome. That target result could conceivably be attained in either of two ways. First, when it is acknowledged that the Pareto-optimum outcome actually realized is what it is because the initial distribution of resource endowments is what it is, redistributions of endowments could be made. The market system could then be left to work out its results on that altered basis. Or second, after the actual or the assumedly Pareto-optimum outcome has been achieved, a redistribution of income or wealth could be made in order to move individuals or classes of individuals to superior welfare positions.

It is clear that virtually unsurmountable obstacles stand in the way of effecting redistributions of initial endowments. For included in those endowments will be certain levels of skills and abilities, knowledge, motivations and other individual characteristics that cannot be redistributed. Conceivably a tax could be placed on superior skills and a distribution of resources thereby made to individuals of lesser endowment. But problems of measurement, quite apart from obvious disincentive effects, make any such proposals irrelevant. For such reasons, arguments designed to improve on unacceptably skewed wealth and welfare distributions have concentrated on effecting changes in actually realized economic and market outcomes.

The compensation principles of Kaldor and Hicks become relevant at that point. They are to be seen in the light of Bergson's ([1938] 1969) concept of a social welfare function, in terms of which he had proposed that comparisons of the relative levels of aggregate social welfare could be made. That function, it was imagined, could be derived from individual preference functions, though a weakness in the proposal lay in the difficulty of discovering any effective means of deriving aggregate utilities from individual utility statements. If, however, a map of such aggregate social indifference curves could be conceptualized in the manner of familiar neoclassical indifference relations, then an aggregative welfare and redistribution argument might be understood to follow.

We might conceive for this purpose of a family of familiar indifference curves, generated from a social welfare function and negatively inclined in a two-dimensional space spanned by the utilities realizable by two different income or social classes. We may introduce into the same space a locus of all attainable Pareto-optimum distributions or outcomes, such as may be achievable on the basis, as already described, of given initial endowments. The question then arises as to which of all the possible attainable Pareto optima is to be regarded as the most favorable or the optimum optimorum. Conceivably, the theory suggests, this most favorable optimum occurs at that point on the locus of possible Pareto optima at which that locus is tangential to the highest attainable social indifference curve. The analytics that follow are consistent with familiar neoclassical utility optimization analysis and do not call for extended discussion at this point.

Arrow's famous "impossibility theorem" subsequently demonstrated that except under extremely stringent conditions it was not possible to derive a unique social preference function (see Arrow [1951] 1963; Rothschild 1993, 78–81). Such a derivation could be made if all individual preferences were identical, a condition, of course, that could hardly be expected to exist in fact. But given the logic of what was involved, the Kaldor-Hicks compensation proposals followed and purported to circumvent some of the difficulties in the aggregate social welfare concept. This they did by focusing on the respects in which the welfare-generating outcomes of different income or social classes or groups might be compared. By appropriately designed taxation and subsidy payments, a redistribution of resources from one class to another could be effected. That would mean that some persons in the first class would be made worse off than before. But the redistribution of resources would alter the production and output potential of the economy as a whole. It might be possible as a result for those who gained from the redistribution to compensate those who were the losers and still realize a higher level of welfare or satisfaction than previously. If, in such a way, there could be an overcompensation, then society as a whole would clearly gain by the redistribution of resources that was contemplated.

Again at that point, however, the question of the grounds of ethical vindication arises. What ethical ground exists, it can then be asked, for the contemplation and the advisability of such a redistributive change. Furthermore, even if a satisfactory answer to that question is assumed, there arises the quite severe difficulty of actually bringing into effect any such change as is envisaged. Politically, any number of barriers, such as the existence of power centers or special interest influence, may stand in the way. Additionally, as Scitovsky (1941) subsequently pointed out, a serious difficulty inheres in the analytical argument and in its redistributive program. It would be necessary in considering any such scheme of resource reallocation to take into account the possible way or ways in which the previously mentioned locus of Pareto optima depend on the technological and institutional conditions that exist or that might be introduced as a result of the redistribution.

It might be possible, in the context of some such redistribution, to introduce new and altered institutional arrangements that shift the attainable locus of Pareto optima outwards in the utility or preference plane. Everybody may thereby be made potentially better off. In that sense, such institutional changes as may be thought to be desirable may make an improved social welfare outcome possible. That may be so, as already indicated, in the sense that once again the gainers in the redistribution are now able to compensate the losers and still remain better off.

But while that result may follow, it may also be true under certain conditions that the redistribution may create the possibility of a completely new locus of Pareto optima and with it the potential for adverse effects. It may be found, for example, that when the new Pareto-optima possibility locus is subjected to the same welfare and potential redistribution analysis as before, the original position from which the first redistribution was made may turn out to be an attainable superior point. In technical terms that can be inspected in the places referred to, the newly created locus of Pareto optima, which is twisted to the new form it assumes by the production potentialities inherent in the redistributed resource endowments and accompanying institutional changes, may intersect the initially established locus. Scitovsky's argument, which introduces in this fashion the potential significance of technological and institutional arrangements, has thus introduced an element of ambiguity to the entire welfare redistribution theory.

It follows that from the point of view of economic analysis the new welfare theoretic program has led to something of an intellectual dead end. But the intellectual experiments that have been involved do point to significant ethical considerations. It is in no sense true that the possession of more material goods, or for society as a whole a larger level of Gross Domestic Product, necessarily implies a higher level of welfare. More things are undoubtedly important for human well-being than the economist has dreamed of. But while that is so, and if for the moment it can be taken that more is better than less, the challenge is clearly laid before economists to consider whether some kind of redistribution, of either resources at one end or of income produced at the other end of the economic process, might conduce to an overall improvement in the social condition. For that purpose any number of grounds of morality, or ethical criteria of the kinds to which we have referred, may again be adduced. At the same time, the Scitovsky propositions point to the possibility of alterations in economic institutional arrangements that might well lead to further improvements in overall social welfare. Such institutional changes might be directed, for example, to the elimination of forms of discrimination, on the basis of color, gender, or national origin. They might be related also to the more widespread provision of improved educational opportunities.

RAWLS'S REDISTRIBUTION PROPOSAL

A number of formal statements of ethical theory that bear on these issues have appeared, such as Rescher's *Distributive Justice* (1966) to which reference was made in a previous chapter, and Rawls's *Theory of Justice* (1971). The latter has generated a considerable critical and evaluative literature (see, for example, Wolff 1977, who refers to Rawls's "puzzling book" that "shifts repeatedly from the most sophisticated deployment of the formal models of economics and mathematics to discussions of outdated topics" (1977, 3; Ball 1986)). Rawls has offered suggestions of a deontic kind for the realization of a morally acceptable, or just, distribution of economic welfare (see also Alejandro 1993).

Much has been made in the critical and evaluative literature of Rawls's proposals to measure well-being by an index of "primary social goods." He explicitly seeks for an "Archimedean point from which the basic structure [of the social system] itself can be appraised" (1971, section 41, excerpted in Hahn and Hollis 1979, 165). The pointedly economic thrust of his argument and the relevance of his proposal for economic distribution stem from his conception of "a class of goods that are normally wanted as parts of rational plans of life" (1979, 165–66) and his notion that the provision of a certain level of "primary social goods" denotes what he refers to as "justice as fairness." It is that "justice as fairness [that] sets up an Archimedean point for assessing the social system" (1979, 166).

In his conception of "a well-ordered society" Rawls imagines that "everyone has a similar sense of justice and in this respect a well-ordered society is homogeneous. Political argument appeals to this moral consensus" (1979, 168; see also the critical evaluation in Ball 1986). Rawls has pointed out in the same context the similarity of his proposition to the notion of the "impartial spectator" of Hume and Smith that we noted in an earlier chapter.

The degree to which Rawls's theory points toward economic equality has also been variously evaluated. That issue is to be seen in the light of what Rawls has referred to as his "difference principle." That principle is so named because it "determines permissible socioeconomic *differences* among people whose shares are otherwise presumed to be equal." In alternative terms, the same proposition is referred to as the "maximin" criterion "because it requires society to distribute goods so as to maximize the minimum possible allotment as compared with possible alternative distributions" (Ball 1986, 226). The distributive criterion is then stated in the following terms.

All social values . . . are to be distributed equally unless an unequal distribution of any, or all, of these values is to everyone's advantage. . . . The higher expectations of those better situated are just if and only if they work as part of a scheme which improves the expectations of the least advantaged. . . . The social order is not to establish and secure the more attractive prospects of those better off unless doing so is to the advantage of those less fortunate. (Rawls 1971, 62, 75, excerpted in Ball 1986, 226)

Departures from equality in economic distribution are thus permissible, and may in fact be desirable, provided distributions can be made in such a way as to "maximize the expectations of the least advantaged" (Wolff 1977, 201).

In his deontic ethical stance Rawls has here taken a position quite different from that of classic utilitarianism. His focus is not simply on the ends that might be realized if participants in the economic process set out to maximize a level of achievable utility, or were to satisfy in an optimal sense a designated preference ordering. Rawls has not based his argument on the classic utilitarian proposition that the benefits of income or wealth redistribution emanate from the supposed realities of diminishing marginal utility. On the contrary, Rawls has shifted the ethical desiderata to focus on a principle that ought, in his view, to be obeyed out of considerations of fairness and justice and as an obligatory behavior criterion.

At the same time, Rawls's primary-goods approach can be criticized on the grounds that more is relevant to the expectations and the economic position of the least advantaged than the possession of goods. Sen, for example, has observed on the importance of the "capabilities" that individuals possess, or the capacity they have to perform desired functions or achieve desired outcomes. Hausman and McPherson, in their discussion of Sen's advance in that respect beyond Rawls, observe that

A capability is the ability to achieve a certain sort of functioning—literacy is a capability; reading is a "functioning." People may value capabilities for their own sake as well as for the functionings they permit—you're glad to know you can walk around even if you are inclined to stay put. (1993, 691)

These various arguments relating to an optimum or an acceptable distribution of income and wealth converge with the earlier concept of Pareto optimality. On Rawls's criteria, for example, a movement to a Pareto-superior distribution, meaning thereby a move that improved one or more individuals' positions and left all others at least as well off as before, would be desirable.

AN ALTERNATIVE SCHEME

Rawls's proposals for "minimum primary goods" or his "difference principle" that countenances certain forms of redistribution can be taken as a starting point for considering the details of ethically acceptable structures. The relevant conception is that of a comparison between the economic positions of the better off in society on the one hand and the worse off on the other. But no necessity appears to be served by insisting, in the manner of Rawls, on an equality of distribution as a base line for comparisons. What is at issue is that to every reasonable extent poverty conditions should be alleviated in a manner that preserves human dignity, at the same time as incentives for individual responsibility and participation in the productive activity of the economy are preserved. Beyond the Rawls prescription, then, both a well-defined ethical principle and an operative guideline or procedure might be contemplated. In pursuing such an agenda it will be clear that again a deontic, as distinct from an exclusively consequentialist, principle determines acceptable ethical criteria.

As an example, a redistributive rule is proposed that defines a minimum acceptable income level to be made available to each employable individual, adjustable in the light of familial and dependent responsibilities. The level at which that minimum benefit is to be established is not intended to be specified at this point. At issue, rather, is simply the statement of the objective that, in accordance with socially acceptable standards consistent with the ethic of solidarity, morally approvable minimum benefits should be preserved. Then the criteria of "justice" or "fairness," to import again the Rawls terminology, are taken to state that only those income redistributions are desirable or required that are necessary to maintain the specified minima. Again at that point the design of suitable taxation and subsidy payments may enter. Or a progressive income tax or a scheme of tax allowances or negative income taxes for non-income earners may be proposed. Or cash subsidy payments that are tied to specific real entitlements, such as housing allowances, might be envisaged.

Such a conception, in a sense, inverts the Rawls criterion. For Rawls has specified that "the social order is not to establish and secure the more attractive prospects of those better off unless doing so is to the advantage of those less fortunate." Rawls, that is, prohibits certain kinds of income and wealth distributions and argues for those that improve the position or the prospects of those who are worse off. Our present rule states that if minimum acceptable conditions are provided for the worse off, understanding again that those conditions are ethically acceptable, then further redistributions are not required and are not necessarily to be called for. The "prospects of those better off" may well, in such circumstances, be improved.

The statement of the ethical implications in that form acknowledges the further ethical mandate of individual responsibility. It is apposite to note, therefore, two further considerations. First, the operative procedure that is involved brings the ethical principle to bear on the condition of what have been termed employable individuals. At issue at that point are the ethic of work and the obligation to work that we raised at the beginning. In recognition of the concomitant demands of that ethic, work effort of one kind or another should be exchanged for the minimum guaranteed income that is provided. In that manner, human dignity will be preserved. Second, it follows that the concept of economic contribution is to be preserved as correlative to that of economic entitlement. The ethic of solidarity, in other words, involves solidarity in economic productive activity as well as solidarity in the participation in economic benefits.

The concept of solidarity is reciprocally interpretable. What is at issue is not a single redistributive ethic, but what might be conceptualized as an ethical matrix. The more difficult task is required, that is, of maintaining mutual consistency between the demands of concomitantly recognized, and cognate and interdependent, ethical principles. Ethical principles of work contribution and individual responsibility, of entitlement sharing under appropriately defined conditions, and of mutual or solidaristic obligations, come to concurrent expression.

It is important to clarify again a principal point at issue. The ethic of redistribution that has been proposed is not designed to address, in the manner of Rawls, distributions that are not permissible unless certain accompanying desiderata are satisfied. It does not envisage, that is to say, distributions that can be permitted only if certain concomitant conditions exist, such as Rawls's notion of fairness in sharing implies. On the contrary, the principle that is proposed states that certain distributions that might otherwise be contemplated do not need to be made when certain conditions, namely the provision of minimum income supports, have been satisfied. It is, alternatively stated, a positive statement regarding redistributions that need to be made in order to satisfy underlying ethical desiderata that are addressed to minimum social and economic conditions.

The principle proposed argues for an economic safety net, not for a necessary equality in economic benefits. It recognizes that individuals are not equal in personal endowments, abilities, ambitions, motivations, income-earning capacity, and the ability to contribute to the economy's total production of benefits. The principle that in this way recognizes economic differentiation is designed to satisfy the ethic of the sanctity of individual property and the freedom of economic use and disposal of it, subject only to certain stated qualifications. These are, first, the address to gross inequities or inequalities of wealth inheritances, and second, the sharing with the less advantaged of the fruits and the benefits of what the employment of property produces.

But given the inseparability, as it is here seen, of the ethic of economic contribution from that of economic entitlement, two implications follow, each of which raises issues of moral dimension. First, if work is called for, a responsibility rests on the political administration to adopt those policies that, there is reason to believe, will make employment opportunities available. This may be done not only in avenues directed to government employment in, say, the construction and maintenance of the economy's infrastructure. Involved also may be economic policies that are designed to improve employment prospects and to make available the necessary education to establish employability in the economy's private sector.

Second, the question arises, as already indicated, of the need to provide taxation revenues that may be necessary to implement such schemes of redistribution or the provision of such work opportunities as are envisaged. Value judgments and ethical proprieties thus enter, in various ways, into the contemplation of the ends of economic and distributive justice and the different possible means that might be proposed to realize them.

It will undoubtedly be the case that minimum income entitlements will need to be made available, at levels consistent with those that have so far been contemplated, to individuals who are unemployable. Clearly, an ethical principle of compassion in solidarity again expresses its demands at that point. In the United States such welfare programs as Aid to Families with Dependent Children (AFDC), food stamps, and entitlements to unemployment benefits can be examined for their economic and cultural viability. Along with the ethics of solidarity in entitlements and contribution, individual responsibility, work, and compassion, it is necessary to have regard to such socio-cultural imperatives as, for example, the preservation of family units.

It is acknowledged that whatever such schemes are adopted, individuals may exploit the system to their advantage, implying the disadvantage of the population whose taxation obligations support the relevant programs. But again, our immediate concern is with the nature of the ethical imperatives that are brought into view, rather than with an extended argument for particular proposals. Suffice it to say that concomitant ethics of integrity call for appropriate and fairly designed safeguards against, and penalties for, exploitation, in the same way as they provide for work or contribution requirements. Again the ethic of contribution is seen in correlation with that of entitlement. An appropriately defined ethical matrix is again brought to consideration.

Ethical responsibility of the kind envisaged will not be able to be discharged without social disruption unless the nature of that responsibility is understood and subscribed to by the members of society at large. We do not make at this point any assumption of homogeneity of individuals and their economic status or ethical preconceptions. Individuals differ. But an aggregative ethical subscription is necessary, not only for improved and generalized social welfare, but also for social stability. Our argument points, therefore, to a collective morality. That comes to expression on several levels.

First, at the same time as the structures of ethical criteria that have been advanced are realized, it will be necessary to acknowledge the ongoing and iterative pressure of them. For as has been said, economic realities eventuate in the context of real historical time, with the surprises and the contradictions of our prescience that it brings. It is not possible, as a result, to effect a once-for-all distribution of endowments and benefits that satisfies ethical desiderata without the need for further adjustment and amendment.

Second, collective morality inheres in the need for economic and social policies to keep the economy on an even keel, growing at a maintainable rate, and providing the opportunities for generalized betterment that have been envisaged. We shall return to a number of relevant questions on these levels in the next chapter, when linkages with the collective ethic will be observed.

IMPLICATIONS FOR ECONOMIC ACTIVITY

It follows from the foregoing argument that in connection with any scheme of income or benefit distribution two significant issues are to be kept in mind. They have to do with, first, the respect in which the levels at which factors of production are rewarded, for example the wage and profit rates, determine the distribution of produced incomes; and second, the manner in which ethical criteria influence judgment as to the acceptability of the income and wealth distributions that result. On the last mentioned point, such considerations as those of Rawls's minimum primary goods criterion and our alternative proposal come to focus and need not be discussed further at this stage. A minimum set of observations can be made, however, on the relevance of factor rewards.

Neoclassical economic theory, expanding the concept of the margin that it inherited from the early nineteenth-century classicists, developed a full-blown theory of the marginal productivity pricing of factors of production. The work of the theologian-economist Philip Wicksteed ([1894] 1932, [1910] 1950) bears scrutiny for its thoroughgoing revisionist statement of the marginalist principles. The concept of productivity at the margin of factor employment set the stage for what became known as the marginal productivity theory of income distribution (see Ferguson 1969; Katzner 1988).

The essentials of that marginal productivity theory of distribution were contained also in J.B. Clark's *Distribution of Wealth* in 1899 (see Spiegel 1991, 618ff.). Clark's work is worthy of inspection in our present context for its suggestion that an ethical propriety attached to the principle of rewarding factors at rates defined by their marginal products. That followed, as Clark saw it, from the supposition that the marginal product, under conditions of perfect competition, measured the social contribution of the factors.

On the level of ethical evaluation, a number of issues arise from this neoclassical fascination with marginal productivity. First, it is difficult to conceive that in fact the requirements of the theory can be satisfied. Consider first the possible relation between the wage rate and the marginal product of labor. In order to define and measure such a marginal product it is logically and mathematically necessary to hold given and constant the amounts of the other factors of production, say capital, with which labor is put to work. An extensive debate followed from Robinson's early expression of concern for the soundness of the neoclassical logic at that point (see Harcourt 1972, 1976). It culminated in the realization that it was not logically possible to measure, as has just been seen to be necessary, the amount of capital in the firm. The notion of capital as a factor of production, in the sense that it is usable for the analytical purposes we have indicated, fell to the ground as a result. It therefore followed that the neoclassical production function argument was circular.

The wage rate, as a result, cannot be regarded as an endogenously determined variable, or, to put it in familiar market terms, as the equilibrating variable in an endogenously clearing labor market. It must be understood, analytically, as an exogenous variable whose magnitude is determined by whatever processes of bargaining are in place. It follows that any attempt, such as might be imagined to be supportable by the neoclassical theory, to establish a linkage between a factor's marginal product and the ethical acceptability of the reward it receives falls to the ground. The ethical propriety of the wage level must therefore be adjudicated on other grounds. That ethical propriety turns on the nature of the bargaining process under which such rates are determined, or, in other words, the distribution of bargaining power between the employer and the employed.

That relative power may change during different phases of the business cycle, and the suppliers of labor may well be able to press more successfully for higher wage rates under conditions of full or near full employment. But two other aspects of the process need also to be taken into account. In the first place, it is conceivable that an excessive concentration of economic power, in the hands of either the employing corporations or the suppliers of labor or their representatives, may lead to the exploitation of that power to the disadvantage of one side or the other. It is not necessary to insist at length on the ethic that is involved at that point.

But second, it is all too clear also that certain sections of the labor force, in what is in fact a highly segmented labor market, may find themselves at acute bargaining disadvantages by reason of discrimination against them. That discrimination, as is empirically and historically observable in the United States industrial complex, may exist on grounds of color, national origin, or gender. Again it is not necessary to address at any length the question of the morality that is involved at that point.

Market morality will in general be furthered by an absence of discrimination, and by as generalized as possible an equality of opportunity. That equality of opportunity extends not only to the market place where the employment of labor is involved, but also to the provision of equality of educational opportunity, medical care, housing, and all types of cultural participation.

On the levels we have addressed, ethical proprieties in the broadest sense are not likely to be served if all market participants, on all sides of the markets, insist only on a self-interested conception of a consequentialist ethic. Quite apart from ethical proprieties, moreover, certain forms of exploitation of power in the interest of self-gratification can point too readily to more widespread economic dislocation. The position of labor, meaning by that executive management as well as hourly paid labor, and its demands for income rewards can be taken as a case in point. The argument to be made spills over to the possible recognition of what we have termed the ethic of solidarity and its wider economic consequences.

The relevant question concerns the manner in which, from time to time, the wage and salary reward of labor is to be adjusted. It was seen in an earlier context that in order to avoid the emergence of inflationary pressures in the economy, the rate of increase in income payments needed to be kept in line with the rate of increase in the ability of the economy to pay such increases. That, it was seen, was determined by the simultaneous increase in the level of productivity in the economy. Without reopening that discussion at length, it brings forcibly to focus the relation between individual accountability, as that is inherent in action in one's own interests at the level we have indicated, and the demands of ethical solidarity, such, for example, as our initial frame of reference has envisaged.

CONCLUDING COMMENT

It has been claimed, particularly by those who emphasize the ethic of voluntary redistribution, that no sustainable mandate could be conceived to exist, on any ethical grounds, for compulsory income or wealth redistribution. The disadvantaged, it is argued, may legitimately benefit from voluntary distributions, but they do not in any sense enjoy any right, or have any moral claim, to receive a share of any other individual's income or wealth. The market system, it is argued on such grounds, can be left to work out its results on the basis of whatever distribution of starting points the market participants enjoy, and the outcomes are to be taken as representing legitimate individual entitlements.

We have pointed to a number of ethical considerations that arise on that level, such as impact on the distribution of initial endowments on the one hand and the redistribution to the disadvantaged of part of the results of the process on the other. Many of the issues that are involved take on an aggregative character and abut more directly the solidarity dimension of our frame of argument. They will therefore be addressed more fully in the following chapter, in which a number of issues on the level of macromorality will be considered.

8 MACROECONOMICS AND MACROMORALITY

Among the ethical tensions and dichotomies that have guided our discussion to this point, those of deontic versus consequentialist criteria, and individuality versus solidarity, have been prominent. The last mentioned comes to relevance now in the consideration of aggregative economic developments and related ethical criteria. In a significant sense, the pressures of a solidaristic ethic have formed our attitudes to the issue of income, wealth, and benefit distribution. Our observations in this chapter will expand that earlier emphasis and will take up some relevant questions of aggregative economic policy.

Moral responsibility attaches to the recognition of the need for economic policies, and to the design and implementation of them. Differences of view exist among economists, of course, regarding the technical nature and potential effectiveness of different policy instruments and alternatives. Indeed, moral and ethical sensitivities, as well as ideological divergences on philosophic and socio-cultural grounds, may dispose different economists toward different policy preferences. That highly significant possibility was canvassed in an earlier chapter in the discussion of the moral content of means versus ends.

But in one way or another, existence and conduct in the aggregate social economy cannot be detached from the pressures of ethical considerations. Our objective in this final chapter is to bring together in a summary fashion a number of relevant questions that deserve recognition.

THE CONCEPTUAL BACKGROUND

Joan Robinson, whose *Economic Philosophy* ends, as we have observed, on the somewhat plaintive "we must not abandon hope," has propelled our thought to the moral dimension of macroeconomics and macroeconomic policy. Her recollection of Cambridge economics can be read in the light of issues we have raised in earlier contexts. "It is true that in Cambridge," she says, "we had never been taught that economics should be *wertfrei* or that the positive and the normative can be sharply divided. We knew that the search was for fruit as well as light. . . . Marshall, certainly, was a great moralizer, but somehow the moral always came out that whatever is, is very *nearly* best" (1962, 74). The "whatever is" that Robinson had in view at that point was the classical conception of laissez faire capitalism, or at least capitalism subject to the constraints and market imperfections that existed. It was as though Pigou, as Robinson recalled him, had got it right when, though he "set out the argument of his *Economics of Welfare* in terms of exceptions to the rule that *laissez faire* ensures maximum satisfaction; he did not question the rule" (idem. loc. cit.).

That very conception, of course, the notion of the classical commitment to laissez faire, was open to significant modification in practice. Apart from the questions that Adam Smith had raised concerning the functional efficiency of an uninhibited market system, the neoclassicists of the last quarter of the nineteenth century were articulately concerned with departures from atomistic competition. The concept of utility and other aspects of their reconstruction of economic theory provided an entry to practical issues of poverty, progressive taxation, and income distribution, and to the practical question of unemployment and public works expenditures (see Hutchison 1978, 257–60 and his judicious summary of, among other things, Pigou's economic policy position). But the questions remain of the presence or otherwise of an explicit morality content, or the recognition of a legitimate place for such a content, in the economic analysis of the late nineteenth and early twentieth centuries.

We have commented at adequate length on the possibility, or, as we have seen it, the impossibility, of a value-free economics, and on the illegitimacy of a rigorous normative-positive distinction. Our dissent was from the early establishment of that dichotomy at the hands of John Neville Keynes, the Cambridge economist whose *Scope and Method of Political Economy* (1891) consolidated the pattern of methodology in the discipline. But Robinson, in her concern for "fruit as well as light" and her sensitivity to a moral imperative, has challenged our sense of historical perspective. She has claimed that "Keynes [John Neville's more brilliant son, John Maynard] brought back the moral problem that *laissez-faire* theory had abolished" (1962, 74).

The sense of morality to which Robinson refers had been awakened by the realization that, if left to itself, the market system would not necessarily and automatically equilibrate at a situation of full employment. The deprivation that unemployment carried with it, when workers were unemployed simply as a result of the malfunctioning of the economic system, disturbed the conscience and controverted the classical economics that had said that such a condition could not occur. Or in many instances a disjunction existed between economists' practical and policy concerns on the one hand, and the analytical constructions that provided the perspectives from which they endeavored to understand and explain the system.

John Maynard Keynes was no doubt on sound ground in setting out not to destroy capitalism, but to rescue it from its malfunctioning deficiencies and to see it, as he said, "wisely managed" and "made more efficient for attaining economic ends" ([1931] 1972, 9:294). The deficiencies of the system, Keynes in due course enabled us to see, did not have to do simply with the clogging rigidities and frictions and market imperfections that distanced the reality from theoretical suppositions regarding it. Harking back to the considerable achievements in analytical economics in the preclassical period, we hear Josiah Child projecting to us the same complaint and plea: "It is our duty to God and nature so to provide for, and employ the poor" (see Vickers 1959, vi). Or perhaps One of old spoke more insightfully than we are ready to acknowledge in his dictum that "the poor you have always with you" (Matt. 26:11).

SOME CONTRIBUTING ECONOMIC ARGUMENTS

Economic realities require it to be borne in mind, in connection, for example, with any proposed scheme of redistribution such as we have suggested, that a relation exists between equity and fairness on the one hand and economic efficiency, or maximum attainable production, on the other. That relation has been addressed in our earlier comments on the locus of attainable Pareto-optimum points. Different distributions, which may be taken to satisfy designated ethical criteria, may be achieved by a redistribution of initial endowments or of realized incomes. But no necessary correlation exists between economic justice and economic efficiency. At issue, however, is the respect in which the interests of economic justice are served by a concern for the ethics of both accountability and solidarity, as they are projected by our earlier frame of reference. An economic society in which the claims of distributive justice are satisfied will not necessarily be the most efficient from the point of view of economic inputs and outputs. And similarly, a technologically most efficient economy will not necessarily satisfy the criteria of justice in distribution.

Economic argument has consistently, certainly since the reformulation of its agenda in the 1930s, made much of the division between microeconomic and macroeconomic analysis. The former has been addressed pointedly to criteria of economic efficiency. It crystallized the theories of production, consumption, value, exchange, and the distribution of income among factors of production at the level of the producing firm. On those levels the concept of the margin became pervasively determinative. It led to theories of marginal productivity of factors of production on the input side, marginal utility or marginal rates of substitution between commodities on the output side, and marginal rates of transformation of one possible output into another via reallocations of resource inputs. In the analytical structure that microeconomics established there was no room, however, for what came to be realized in due course as the macroeconomic problem. That refers to the fact that no inherent reason existed why the relations between inputs and outputs would necessarily lead to the full employment of all of the available factors of production. A worrying logical and empirical hiatus came to be recognized between microeconomics and what was, as a result, labeled macroeconomic analysis.

On the level of morality, the problem that thus gained recognition was that among the resources that might be left unemployed by the operation of the market system was the human resource of labor. Of course to the extent to which, in the analysis of the economic system and its potentialities, reliance was placed on the assumptions of Say's Law, the possible unemployment problem could be assumed away. For Say's Law implied that all of the incomes generated in producing the national product would be spent, in one way or another, in purchasing the national product. What was not spent in purchasing consumption goods, it was supposed, would automatically flow into the purchase of investment goods, thereby implying higher levels of capital formation in the economy. As a result, there could not exist any deficiency of demand for what the economy was capable of producing, and there could not exist, therefore, any deficiency of demand for factors of production, including, notably, labor, that were employable to produce the national product.

But those halcyon, harmonious conditions, it was in due course seen, would not necessarily be realized. Keynes had seen the possibility, to put the issue in the words of John Locke as he had crystallized it as early as 1691, that "the money of the nation may lie dead, and thereby prejudice trade" ([1691] 1870, 226). The microeconomic assumption that interdependent market forces would automatically lead to an everywhere consistent market clearing meant that in the outcome all market participants would be somewhere on their demand and supply curves. Being there, they would be where their utility functions told them they wanted to be. But if that were so, then it could be concluded that in the market for labor the suppliers of labor were also on their aggregate supply curve, and any unemployment that existed would therefore be voluntary unemployment. The involuntary unemployment problem was solved by assuming it away.

An issue of morality clearly protruded from what therefore followed as the awareness of the macroeconomic problem. Workers might well become unemployed, not through any fault of their own or because of a disinclination to work. Unemployment might be due simply to the sheer malfunctioning and the dynamics of the economic system. But in some contemporary systems of economic analysis the assumption is inherent that Say's Law is again at work. The economy is imagined, that is, to tend to settle automatically at a position of full employment. To the extent that that is so, the involuntary unemployment problem is again assumed away. The condition of full employment is, of course, variously defined, and in some modern expressions it has been understood as the "natural rate of unemployment" to which, by virtue of market clearing conditions in the market for labor, the system automatically tends. In such directions, the so-called new classical economics, which incorporates the assumption of rapid market adjustment velocities as well as that of rational expectations, fairly completely rehabilitates the classical market analysis.

In analytical thought systems that in ways such as these minimize the possibility of a less than satisfactory functioning of the macroeconomy, the pressure for the recognition of what we have called an ethic of solidarity is minimized. A significant body of thought, which has lately emerged as a revival of what has been referred to as Austrian economics, also bears in an interesting fashion on the issues we now have in view. The neo-Austrian economics has imagined that notwithstanding difficulties of information transmission, the market system will in general tend to achieve a full employment level of operation. It rests its claims on what, following Hayek (1949), is understood as a condition of equilibrium that the economy reaches as a result of a coordination or compatibility between the activity plans of all market participants. In that sense neo-Austrianism takes what has been called a teleological view of the market. The market tends, that is, to realize a teleological objective, that of the full employment of resources. The Austrian economists O'Driscoll and Rizzo speak of "pattern coordination" or plan coordination as an approach to the meaning of equilibrium (1985, 85ff.; see also Davidson 1989).

Austrianism, moreover, generally assumes an analytical focus on microeconomic market analysis, to the neglect of macroeconomics. Not only is it claimed that macroeconomic behavior functions cannot be defined in a satisfactory logical sense. In view of the difficult process of information coordination in the economy, it is said that macroeconomic policies are likely to be rendered ineffective, if, indeed, their implementation is not in danger of worsening what problems of macroeconomic coordination exist. The issue of immediate relevance, however, is that a system of thought that sets aside the problem of a less than satisfactory functioning of the aggregate economy is not likely to address in a significant manner what we have called the ethic of macromorality. The ethic of solidarity,

to employ again our alternative terminology, is not in such a thought system likely to come into adequate relation with the ethic of individual
accountability.

Contemporary fashions in economic theorizing have returned extensively and intensively to the analytics of microeconomics. In the newer
forms of so-called new-Keynesian theory, analysis is focused again on
micromarket processes, and primary attention is given to reasons why market rigidities and empirical frictions inhibit the smoother realization of
more satisfactory aggregate outcomes. It is necessary for the formation of
logically coherent thought schemes, it is thus widely claimed, to investigate
and establish a sound microeconomic foundation under whatever macroeconomic arguments or proposals are advanced. That implies that economic argument in general is not thought to be logically maintainable
unless it is grounded in the description of optimizing behavior on the part
of individual economic agents.

That important methodological issue aside for the present, however, it
does need to be observed that in the same way as an economics of individual behavior stands in potential relation to aggregative or macroeconomic
analysis, so also on the level of ethical theory and desirable moral action an
individual or microethic stands in potential relation to issues of macromorality. In the case of ethical criteria, moreover, the microethic is to be
seen as prior, in both a logical and a causal sense, to the issue of aggregate
or system-wide morality.

MICROETHICS AND MACROMORALITY

The ethic of individual accountability emanates from the conception of
stewardship over the endowments of resources, abilities, and opportunities
with which the individual is entrusted. Let it be imagined that a definable
distribution of endowments exists. Or, alternatively, such a distribution
may have been brought into existence by a reallocation such as was envisaged in the previous chapter. The question that is heavily laden with ethical import, then, is that of what a given individual will do in the
management of the resources over which he or she has command. Ethical
responsibility and, as we have now put it, ethical accountability exist on a
number of readily recognizable levels.

First, it can be asked, what is the direction of employment to which
resources will be put? Second, what is the degree of integrity with which
those resources are utilized for the purposes in view? Third, what is the
manner in which, and the level at which, attempts are made to extract from
the economic market system fair and sustainable rewards for the utilization
of those resources? Fourth, what is the manner in which the rewards thus
obtained, or the incomes and wealth that are realized as a result of economic activity, are utilized? They may be allocated between immediate

consumption and saving, they affect the structure of consumption demands, and they influence the direction in which saving is invested.

The criteria of ethical behavior on each of these individual levels have already been adequately implied. Individual conduct may be informed by the narrowest of self-interested concern. Or on the other hand, while remaining committed to what we have termed a consequentialist ethic, such conduct might recognize deontic pressures or a sense of ethical obligation. Again that deontic sense might take up the obligations of commitment and sympathy in the fashion of Adam Smith and A.K. Sen. Or it may have greater or lesser regard to implications for aggregate or system-wide conduct and results.

Among the points at which, in such a manner, the ethic of individual conduct impinges on economic outcomes is that relating to the business firm's establishment of labor and employment contracts. The literature directed to the concept of efficiency wage rates was noted in an earlier chapter. What is at issue is the fact that the wage contract cannot in general specify the level and quality of work effort that will actually be supplied on the job. The wage contract generally deals in explicit terms with hours of work, at the same time, of course, as any number of work rules are contemplated and incorporated. But room clearly exists for varying degrees of conscientiousness and performance levels on the part of individual workers. An ethic of obligation comes to focus as a result.

Beyond that, industrial costs of production will be affected by worker performance, including the effect of costs involved in supervisory management and costs of quality control and of possibly defective workmanship. It is clear, therefore, that attainable levels of production and economic efficiency, along with their implications for industrial costs and market selling prices, are potentially affected by individual attitudes to what are interpretable as ethical obligations, responsibility, and accountability.

The individual ethic that underpins the performance, efficiency, and system-wide outcomes of the economy exists also at the point of individuals' allocation of incomes to saving or to consumption expenditure, meaning by that both the level and the commodity structure of expenditure. Two minimal comments will illustrate what might be involved.

First, the structure of consumption expenditure can be judged against standards of morality. That is so to the extent that it affects the discharge of responsibility for the well-being of family dependents and one's own physical, psychological, and cultural health. Second, the wisdom of one's making provision for the future, to the extent that it is possible in the context of earned income to do so, can be raised to the level of moral obligation. For quite apart from the personal and individual considerations that are involved, the cost to the larger economy of making provision for old age support services, not excluding the cost of medical care, clearly involves a burden that might be alleviated by higher levels of individual responsibility.

In ways such as these, the microethic of individual responsibility and accountability lies behind the attainable levels of aggregate national production and the distribution of it. For on one level, the distribution of resources will influence the structure of national production and activity, by reason that different individuals have different skills with which resources can be put to work, and different preferences, motivations, and aspirations. On another level, the distribution of resources will influence the efficiency levels at which the economy operates. It will at the same time determine the level of aggregate national product that is achievable, and thereby the scope for distributive shares that results. While that is so, the totality of individual decisions as to the consumption demands they make on the economy, whether or not those demands might be thought, on some criteria, to be pointlessly conspicuous, has clear implications for the rate of growth in national income and welfare.

ETHICAL IMPERATIVES AND MACROECONOMIC POLICY

The New Welfare Economics, though its ambitious agenda of escape from the utilitarianism of the earlier Pigouvian theory ran into an intellectual dead end, did alert the economics discipline to a number of important issues. First, it might well be possible to conceive of ways in which a redistribution of income or resources from one income class to another held promise of improvement in the general human condition. Second, such a redistribution might be made in a manner that raised the endowments of the lesser advantaged with a view to allowing the market system to work out its untrammeled effects from that point onward. Or alternatively, the redistribution might focus on a relative leveling of the incomes that the otherwise unhindered market process generated. Third, attention was given to certain detailed policies that might be designed to achieve such ends as were envisaged. Alternative taxation and subsidy policies, including, for example, negative income taxes directed toward the lower income classes, were discussed. On the same level it would be possible to consider also proposals for variations in tax rate progressions and exemption allowances, the relative merits of cash endowments and the provision of vouchers for the purchase of such items as food necessities, and subsidies for housing accommodation.

Our immediate concern is with the nature of the ethical imperatives that are relevant to the prospects for the betterment of the human condition. That betterment might be accomplished, it may be thought, by any number or combination of macroeconomic policies. But some political economists have argued, as we noted in an earlier discussion of claims for the sanctity and inviolability of personal property rights, that no moral or philosophic grounds do or can exist for the redistribution of income or wealth endowments. Such advocates frequently hold to the notion that automatic harmonies exist in the economic system adequate to guarantee the attainment of a high and satisfactory level of general economic welfare, and that all will work out for the best if only those in authority concentrate on doing nothing to interfere with the untrammeled working of the system. But reality belies the claim.

In latter day economic reasoning, returning as it has substantially to the automatic harmony assumptions that informed the classical system of thought, the claim is again made that the unemployment problem can be assumed away. Say's Law has enjoyed a reincarnation, money is again neutral, earlier assumptions of perfect knowledge are rehabilitated in the stochastic analog of rational expectations, and whatever unemployment exists is again voluntary unemployment. The economy settles, it is supposed in that newer system of thought, at a natural rate of unemployment.

That natural rate of unemployment is what it is because it is determined by the mutually consistent clearing of all markets in the economy. If it should be observed, as has been the case in recent times, that the level of unemployment at which the economy appears to settle has increased, then the somewhat dismissive explanation is proffered that the natural rate of unemployment has risen. In recent times, then, the natural rate of unemployment appears to have risen each time the economy has emerged from a business cycle recession. It is a scandal on the economics discipline to conclude that nothing can be done to achieve better outcomes on both the unemployment and the price inflation fronts, and to conclude, as a result, that the poor and the unemployed have to be where they are in order to keep the rest of the economy stable and stably productive.

If, then, as is here proposed, an ethic of work and individual responsibility exists in correlation with that of basic benefit entitlement, a collective ethic enforces an obligation on those in authority and in a position to do so to make work available to the population at large.

If it were the case that the economy, if left to itself, would automatically generate a condition of full employment, the pressure of the redistributive ethic we have advanced would be considerably diminished, if not nullified. Of course, even under the best of such idealized conditions there could be expected to be, at any given time, a certain amount of unemployment in the economy. That could be expected to be a natural feature of a dynamic economic system, in which technological possibilities, production arrangements, and product demands were changing. Under those conditions a certain amount of frictional unemployment might be expected to occur as individuals changed jobs and moved to better employment avenues and prospects. The pull of the profit motive would, in a dynamic economy, more or less continually reallocate capital investment and would generate along with it new structures of employment of the economy's workforce. Such frictional unemployment would not only imply potential improvements in human betterment, but it would, it may be hoped, be of short duration as the labor force was being reallocated. No one individual, that is, would need to be unemployed for any significant length of time.

But in the economic system as we know it, such frictional unemployment is not the only kind of dislocation with which we must reckon. On one level, cyclical variations in employment also occur from time to time, emanating from underlying business cycle fluctuations. Those fluctuations do not stem simply from imperfections in market systems or obstacles to rapid adjustment. At that point the need exists to understand the nature of economic shocks that can and do disrupt the even tenor of things for extended periods of time. Prospects for a diminution of the rate of growth of consumer demand, for example, might generate magnified fluctuations in the rate of investment expenditure and capital formation in the economy. The economists' acceleration principle may come into play in a damagingly reverse fashion. Or technological change may turn demand, and therefore employment opportunities, away from certain kinds of products to others. Or reassessments of longer term prospects may induce expenditure decision makers to raise their liquidity preference and hold resources in liquid or money form rather than spend. In such conditions, reductions in expenditure streams generate reductions in incomes, deviation amplifying feedbacks occur, multiplier effects take over, and economic dislocation widens.

The possibility of cyclical unemployment raises the likelihood that welfare provision of the kind we have already envisaged is necessary. In addition to the possibilities of such frictional and cyclical unemployment, moreover, the possibility exists of structural dislocations that generate structural unemployment. A generalized decision in the economy to reduce the importance of coal as a source of energy has led to structural unemployment and deprivation in the coal-producing region of Appalachia in the United States. The construction of an efficient highway system and motorized transportation have led to the relative decline of the railroad industry, in the same way as the railroads earlier displaced canal transportation. Computers have displaced typewriters. Automated assembly lines in automobile production have changed the structure of employment opportunities. Excessive demands for increases in income payments have been thought to generate an inflationary pressure that reduces international competitiveness and dislocates export industries. The possible instances could be multiplied.

For all of these and other analytical reasons that might be adduced, the macroeconomic problem is more profound than simply that of recognizing that the economy automatically settles at what was noted as a natural rate of unemployment. Even, of course, if that were the case, considerations of macromorality would argue against accepting complacently the level of natural unemployment that was envisaged. It is difficult to reconcile the reality, on the one hand, of seven to ten million unemployed employable individuals and, on the other, the need to improve the economy's infra-structure, arrest the urban decay, and provide the reeducation and retrain-ing that the dynamics of technological advance demands. But perhaps an inadequate cultural grasp of the collective ethic that is involved stands in the way of more generalized human betterment.

POLICY INSTRUMENTS

A minimal comment can be made on economic policies that might con-tribute to the human betterment we have envisaged. As is here argued, a collective morality transcends the technical issues of economic policy alternatives. The imperative exists to direct economic policy, not only to the stabilization of economic activity and employment and the generation of maintainable economic growth, but also to a consideration of the human condition that is involved. The moral imperative is imposed on policy mak-ers to attempt to mitigate the human distresses that come into view and bedevil the market economies.

The imperatives of macromorality call for the judicious use of the pol-icy instruments and possibilities that, to its credit, the economics discipline has developed. Monetary policy might be used to keep the economy on course, even though differences of judgment among economists may arise as to the proper timing and effectiveness of monetary policy changes. The responsible authority, the Federal Reserve Board in the United States, may move to raise interest rates too soon in an economic recovery and may cut off the economy's forward progress before it gets sufficiently under way. Or the Federal Reserve Board may act wisely in using monetary pol-icy to cut off the excesses of a boom in order to avoid the distresses of a slump that it might otherwise expect will occur. Differences of judgment occur. But at issue in our present context is the fact that in all such policy actions the need exists to accommodate the demands and the objectives of the collective ethic that has been raised.

On the level of monetary policy, the ethic of concern for the unem-ployed and the relatively disadvantaged can be damaged by misunder-standings regarding the modus operandi of monetary policy effects. There may exist, that is, a defective view of the structure of the transmission channels through which monetary policy transmits its effects to and through the financial and the real markets of the economy. It has fre-quently been imagined, for example, that inflation is substantially a matter of too much money chasing too few goods. The cure for inflation, if that should be the dragon disrupting the economy, is then, from that point of view, simply a reduction in the money supply or in the rate of growth in the money supply. But reductions in the money supply are not likely to have an impact effect on the price level at all. Rather, they are likely to impact most directly on the levels of expenditure and employment. Industrial prices are more likely to depend on the extent to which producers have marked up their unit production costs, and any moderation of prices or price increases that follows the reduction in the money supply will be a delayed response to goods market conditions. In the meantime, the welfare disruptions that accompany unemployment may be worsened as a result of underlying policy misconceptions.

The possibilities of fiscal policy also point directly to the demands of the collective ethic. That is so in several respects. First, the level of government expenditure and the resulting absorption of economic resources by the public sector potentially entail a competition for resources with the private sector of the economy. To the extent that unemployed resources exist, the pressure of that competition for resources is, of course, diminished. Indeed, it is one of the sorriest fallacies of economic argument that public sector spending necessarily crowds out private sector expenditure. Whether it does or does not depends on the state of the economy at the time such a fiscal policy is introduced. To the extent that government expenditure does increase, unconscionable budget deficits may emerge and the competition for resources may worsen unless increases in taxation rates are imposed in order to enhance revenues. At that point, then, the question arises whether the public is willing to provide the revenue that is necessary to enable the government's economic policy to do what it is agreed, in recognition of the collective ethic, needs to be done. That is the crunch point of collective ethical responsibility.

In various ways, the pressure of the collective ethic impinges on the expenditure side of the government's budget also. Direct expenditures are involved in such programs as the Aid to Families with Dependent Children, unemployment compensation, and food stamps. Further, policy decisions to provide subsidies to certain forms of production, as part of a program of welfare and benefit redistribution, also involve direct expenditures. At that point again, moreover, judgments of a clearly ethical kind arise. It remains to be judged, for example, whether the policies of price supports for certain grain products do contribute significantly to desirable welfare redistributions, whether they provide aid in the form of income support to small farmers, or whether they channel funds predominantly to larger and relatively profitable corporate farming enterprises. In ways such as these, the need is raised for judicious investigation of both the objectives and the structural impacts of centralized fiscal policy programs. Finally on the expenditure side of fiscal policy, the question remains whether welfare objectives are not more effectively served by federal government payments to state and local authorities, who might then be charged with welfare distribution, than by the federal government's direct participation in welfare programs.

Fiscal policy is very much concerned with the structure of taxation as well as its level. Revenue policy, as does expenditure policy, may address directly the redistribution objectives that are envisaged. Progressive tax rate scales, exemption allowances for family and child support, housing accommodation, housing construction and finance, incentives for urban development, motivations for individual saving, and fiscal incentives to make provision for retirement are only some examples of the ways in which revenue structures may address larger welfare objectives.

At the same time, considerations of welfare distribution are implicit in decisions regarding the division of the total tax revenue burden between individual income taxation, corporate taxation, and indirect or commodity taxation. Questions of disincentives may well be implicit in one form of taxation or the other. But quite apart from considerations of equity and the relative sharing of burdens that are inherent in the collective ethic we have addressed, technical issues do influence judgments in all of those respects. The burden as distinct from the incidence of commodity taxation, for example, may depend on the market elasticities of supply and demand for the commodities concerned, and the extent to which corporate taxes are transmitted to the consumer might be debatable. In general, regressive taxes, or those that impose a relatively larger burden on lower income earners, should be avoided.

The demands of the collective ethic or macromorality touch in these various ways numerous levels and areas of economic policy. Policies directed to ecological preservation and pollution control have a potential implication for quality of life and general social welfare. Manpower policy and industrial location and regulation are also relevant. From the point of view of generalized welfare it may be argued that discrimination in employment, whether on grounds of color, national origin, or gender, should be eliminated. But that in itself, of course, raises issues of potentially difficult ethical resolution. Legitimate criteria of merit, competitiveness, and efficiency, or even nepotism, may come into contact with more generalized principles of nondiscrimination. A sensible, if delicate, balancing of options and distributions of benefits may clearly be called for in specific instances, at the same time as discrimination for its own sake is prohibited.

Further, the objectives that are here in view are likely to be realized more readily if provision is made for the reeducation and training of displaced members of the workforce. Information regarding employment opportunities can be made readily available through a network of employment exchanges. Assistance in relocation of the workforce can be provided through tax deductions for moving expenses and the availability of affordable interest rate loans.

Less directly, the general welfare as well as the economic status of the workforce is potentially affected by the possibilities inherent in the economy's incomes policy. By that term it is intended to refer to those institutional arrangements that are designed to preserve a satisfactory relation between the rate of change, conceivably increases, in the level of income payments and the concomitant change in the average level of productivity in the economy. If the former rate tends to exceed the latter, then commodity price pressure and possibly a spiraling inflation are likely to result.

The possible avoidance of inflation, so far as that may be achieved by appropriate economic policies, does itself raise issues of ethical import. Immorality attaches to economic policies that permit or encourage the erosion of real incomes and asset values by continued inflation. Immorality attaches also to policies that use deliberately generated unemployment as a weapon against inflation. That policy dilemmas abound on all of these levels is clear. That economic theory has not advanced to the point of assuring their easy or continual resolution is also clear. But at issue at present is the fact that the ethical content of policy obligations does call for their ongoing recognition, and the economics discipline confronts the challenge to achieve higher levels of theoretical understanding and effectiveness in policy prescription.

In the matter of inflation control, proposals have been made from time to time for tax-based incomes policies, envisaging the imposition of taxes on those business firms that pay wage and salary increases at a rate in excess of productivity enhancements. Problems of definition and measurement arise in all such schemes. But such considerations impact on the ethical issues we have addressed at the level at which unsustainable competition for income shares develops. It is a short step from the technicalities of industrial employment and pricing problems to the recognition that if all income classes are simultaneously raising their demands for income increases, then the ability of the economy to pay must depend on the rate at which the economy's total production and income can be raised. If that relation is not maintained at a satisfactory level, disruptions to industrial production costs and commodity price levels can be expected to follow. At that highly significant point an ethic of greed, on the part of those who demand income increases or those who administer price mark-ups in production costs in the interest of enhanced profit rates, can have all too clearly disruptive effects on inflation potentials and diminished social welfare.

Industrial location and regulation policies again contain potential implications for welfare and for the possible alleviation of social distress and dislocation. Official incentives for the relocation of industry to otherwise depressed areas, or to areas where a suitably skilled workforce is available, may take the form of tax incentives, rapid depreciation allowances, low interest rate loans, the formation of financial institutions to channel equity capital to such areas, and the provision of infrastructure facilities.

More extensive areas of potential welfare effects exist at the economic policy level than it is necessary to advert to at length. But the admittedly difficult policy issues and possibilities, while they are seriously and honestly appraised, should not be allowed to cloud the basic fact that a responsibility of collective ethic rests on the decision making authority at the policy level and on the collective citizenry. Called for are maximum ethical awareness and the widest cultivation of moral sensitivities.

CONCLUDING COMMENT

Two final observations reside more directly on the level of moral philosophy or of ethical theory with which we began. A brief reference to them will complete our discussion.

First, the order and emphasis of our argument has deliberately slanted attention to what, to invoke the meta-ethical vocabulary we established at the beginning, is a substantially deontological emphasis. Our ethical perspective has intended to lay emphasis in the first place on the notion of individual accountability. Accountability, of course, could logically be conceived to be accountability to whatever was necessary to achieve desired ends or contemplated objectives. In that case the very concept of accountability would carry with it a consequentialist connotation. But for the main part of our argument, our recognition of the stewardship responsibilities of individuals in their economic positions and relations has envisaged an ethic of obligation and of duty consistent with desiderata other than those of a narrow self-interested objective. That primary emphasis has been implicit both in the parallel conception of solidarity that itself has come to expression on numerous levels and in the arguments that have been advanced for redistributive justice.

Second, it would be a mistake to imagine that all that has been said is directed only to understanding or prescribing for an ideal economic and socio-cultural condition. On the contrary, it is recognized that economic society is subject to all the defects of fallen human nature, and that selfishness, cruelty, greed, lust, discrimination, and exploitation abound. Legislation must accordingly be legislation for a grossly defective human society in what is no doubt a lamentably defective complex of ethical awareness. But any prospects that might be held for human improvement and progress demand all too clearly that as an economic society we do better, on the level of ethical awareness and moral insight, than we have done.

Our enquiry began with the recognition that a relationship existed between culture and morality, as well as between money and commerce. The concept of culture was sharpened at the beginning to focus our attention on its ethical dimension. But there are other cultural forces that warrant investigation. It is a largely unwritten essay that sorts out the economics of the widely different levels of human culture, though some important and instructive tentative incursions have been made (see, for example, Baumol and Bowen 1966). The fear is legitimate, however, that on the level on which we have pursued our discussions, our discipline has been substantially delinquent in the cultivation of conversation with the moral philosophers.

It is nevertheless true, as we noted Walsh earlier to have observed, that "the supposed . . . barriers to fruitful exchange between economic theory and moral philosophy . . . are down, and the honest confrontation of the issues which properly concern the moral sciences can relieve economists from the shameful pretense of ethical neutrality" (1987, 3:868). There is much to be done, and much that is potentially highly rewarding in the task, to quote the title of McPherson's engaging essay, of "Reuniting Economics and Philosophy" (1988, 71–87). Happily, the intellectual climate is changing more rapidly, and as McPherson observes, there is no longer need for economists "to regard any hint of moral judgment in their work as a derogation of professional standards."

REFERENCES

Abegglen, J.C. and G. Stalk. 1988. *Kaishu: The Japanese Corporation*. New York: Basic Books.

Alejandro, R. 1993. "Rawls's Communitarianism." *Canadian Journal of Philosophy* 23, no. 1:75–99.

Aoki, M. 1990. *Information, Incentives, and Bargaining in the Japanese Economy*. Cambridge: Cambridge University Press.

Archibald, G.C. 1959. "Welfare Economics, Ethics, and Essentialism." *Economica* 26:316–27.

Arrow, K.J. [1951] 1963. *Social Choice and Individual Values*. New York: Wiley and Yale University Press.

_____. 1971. *Essays in the Theory of Risk-Bearing*. Chicago: Markham.

Arrow, K.J. and F.H. Hahn. 1971. *General Competitive Analysis*. San Francisco: Holden-Day.

Ball, S.W. 1986. "Economic Equality: Rawls versus Utilitarianism." *Economics and Philosophy* 2, no. 2:225–44.

Baumol, W.J. 1967. *Business Behavior, Value and Growth*. New York: Harcourt, Brace & World.

Baumol, W.J. and W.G. Bowen. 1966. *Performing Arts: The Economic Dilemma*. New York: Twentieth Century Fund.

Becker, G.S. 1976. *The Economic Approach to Human Behavior*. Chicago: University of Chicago Press.

_____. 1981. *A Treatise on the Family*. Cambridge, MA: Harvard University Press.

Bentham, J. 1954. *Economic Writings*. 3 vols. Ed. W. Stark. London: Allen & Unwin.

Bergson, A. [1938] 1969. "A Reformulation of Certain Aspects of Welfare Economics." *Quarterly Journal of Economics* 52:310–34. Reprinted in K. Arrow and T. Scitovsky, eds. *Readings in Welfare Economics.* Homewood, IL: Irwin.

Bernoulli. D. [1738] 1968. "Exposition of a New Theory of Risk Evaluation." In W.J. Baumol and S.M. Goldfeld, eds. *Precursors in Mathematical Economics: An Anthology.* London: London School of Economics and Political Science.

Blanchard, O.J. and S. Fischer. 1989. *Lectures on Macroeconomics.* Cambridge, MA: MIT Press.

Blaug, M. 1980. *The Methodology of Economics: Or How Economists Explain.* Cambridge: Cambridge University Press.

Boland, L.A. 1982. *The Foundations of Economic Method.* London: Allen & Unwin.

Bonar, J. [1885] 1924. *Malthus and His Work.* London: Allen & Unwin.

———. 1893. *Philosophy and Political Economy.* London: Swan Sonnenschein.

Boulding, K.E. 1958. *Principles of Economic Policy.* Englewood Cliffs, NJ: Prentice-Hall.

Bowles S. and H. Gintis. 1993. In S. Bowles, H. Gintis, and B. Gustafsson, eds. *Markets and Democracy: Participation, Accountability, and Efficiency.* Cambridge: Cambridge University Press.

Brandt, R.B., ed. 1961. *Value and Obligation.* New York: Harcourt Brace.

———, ed. 1962. *Social Justice.* Englewood Cliffs, NJ: Prentice-Hall.

Branson, W.H. 1989. *Macroeconomic Theory and Policy.* New York: Harper & Row.

Brown, V. 1991. "Signifying Voices: Reading the 'Adam Smith Problem.'" *Economics and Philosophy* 7, no. 2:187–220.

Buchanan, A. 1985. *Ethics, Efficiency, and the Market.* Totowa, NJ: Rowman & Allenheld.

Caldwell, B. 1982. *Beyond Positivism: Economic Methodology in the Twentieth Century.* London: Allen & Unwin.

———, ed. 1984. *Appraisal and Criticism in Economics: A Book of Readings.* Boston: Allen & Unwin.

Cantillon, R. [1734] 1931. *Essai sur la nature du commerce en général.* English translation, Ed. H. Higgs. London: Macmillan.

Clark, G.H. 1992. *Essays on Ethics and Politics.* Jefferson, NJ: Trinity Foundation.

Clark, J.B. [1899] 1956. *The Distribution of Wealth.* New York: Kelley.

Davidson, P. 1983. "The Marginal Product Curve Is Not the Demand Curve for Labor and Lucas's Labor Supply Function Is Not the Supply Curve for Labor in the Real World." *Journal of Post Keynesian Economics* 6, no. 1:105–17.

———. 1988. "A Technical Definition of Uncertainty and the Long-run Non-neutrality of Money." *Cambridge Journal of Economics* 12, no. 3:329–37.

———. 1989. "The Economics of Ignorance or Ignorance of Economics." *Critical Review* 3, no. 3 and no. 4:467–87.

———. 1991. "Is Probability Theory Relevant for Uncertainty? A Post Keynesian Perspective." *Journal of Economic Perspectives* 5, no. 1:129–43.

de Finetti, B. [1937] 1964. "Foresight: Its Logical Laws, Its Subjective Sources." In H.E. Kyberg et al., eds. *Studies in Subjective Probability*. New York: Wiley.

Dempsey, B.W. [1935] 1960. "Just Price in a Functional Economy." *American Economic Review* 25:471–86. Reprinted in J.J. Spengler and W.R. Allen, eds. *Essays in Economic Thought: Aristotle to Marshall*. Chicago: Rand McNally.

Diamond, P. and M. Rothschild, eds. 1978. *Uncertainty in Economics: Readings and Exercises*. New York: Academic Press.

Duesenberry, J.S. 1949. *Income, Saving and the Theory of Consumer Behavior*. Cambridge, MA: Harvard University Press.

Dupuit, A.J. [1844] 1952. "On the Measurement of the Utility of Public Works." Trans. R.H. Barback. *International Economic Papers* 2:83–110.

Dworkin, G., G. Bermant, and P.G. Brown. 1977. *Markets and Morals*. Washington: Hemisphere Publishing Corporation.

Eatwell, J., M. Milgate, and P. Newman, eds. 1987. *The New Palgrave: A Dictionary of Economics*. 4 vols. London: Macmillan.

Edgeworth, F.Y. 1881. *Mathematical Psychics: An Essay on the Application of Mathematics to the Moral Sciences*. London: Kegan Paul.

Eliot, T.S. 1940. *The Idea of a Christian Society*. New York: Harcourt Brace.

———. 1949. *Notes Towards the Definition of Culture*. New York: Harcourt Brace.

Elster, J. 1989. "Social Norms and Economic Theory." *Journal of Economic Perspectives* 3, no. 4:99–117.

Elster, J. and J.E. Roemer. 1993. *Interpersonal Comparisons of Well-Being*. Cambridge: Cambridge University Press.

Etzioni, A. 1986. "The Case for a Multiple-Utility Conception." *Economics and Philosophy* 2:2,159–83.

Ferguson, C.E. 1969. *The Neoclassical Theory of Production and Distribution*. Cambridge: Cambridge University Press.

Fisher, I. 1927. "A Statistical Method for Measuring Marginal Utility." In J.H. Hollander, ed. *Economic Essays in Honor of J.B. Clark*. New York: Macmillan.

Flux, A.W. 1894. Review of P.H. Wicksteed's *Coordination of the Laws of Distribution*. *Economic Journal* 4:305–13.

Foot, P., ed. 1967. *Theories of Ethics*. Oxford: Oxford University Press.

Fraad, H., S. Resnick, and R. Wolff. 1989. "For Every Knight in Shining Armor, There's a Castle Waiting to be Cleaned: A Marxist-Feminist Analysis of the Household." *Rethinking Marxism* 2:4,9–69.

Friedman, M. 1953. *Essays in Positive Economics*. Chicago: University of Chicago Press.

———. 1962. *Capitalism and Freedom*. Chicago: University of Chicago Press.

———. 1968. "The Role of Monetary Policy." *American Economic Review* 78, no. 1:1–17.

Galbraith, J.K. 1958. *The Affluent Society*. Boston: Houghton Mifflin.

Galiani, F. [1750] 1977. *Della Moneta (Of Money)*. Trans. P.R. Toscano. Ann Arbor: University Microfilms International.

Georgescu-Roegen, N. 1966. *Analytical Economics: Issues and Problems*. Cambridge, MA: Harvard University Press.

Gewirth, A. [1972] 1976. "Moral Rationality." *In Freedom & Morality*, Ed. J. Bricke. Lawrence: University of Kansas Press.

———. 1978. *Reason and Morality*. Chicago: University of Chicago Press.

———. 1982. *Human Rights: Essays on Justification and Applications*. Chicago: University of Chicago Press.

———. 1984. "Ethics." In M.J. Adler et al., eds. *The New Encyclopaedia Britannica*, 15th edition. 6:976–98.

Gossen, H.H. [1854] 1983. *The Laws of Human Relations and the Rules of Human Action Derived Therefrom*. Trans. R.C. Blitz. Cambridge, MA: MIT Press.

Graaf, J. de V. 1957. *Theoretical Welfare Economics*. Cambridge: Cambridge University Press.

Hahn, F. 1982. "On Some Difficulties of the Utilitarian Economist." In A. Sen and B. Williams, eds. *Utilitarianism and Beyond*.

Hahn, F. and M. Hollis, eds. 1979. *Philosophy and Economic Theory*. Oxford: Oxford University Press.

Halevy, E. [1928] 1955. *The Growth of Philosophic Radicalism*. Trans. M. Morris. Boston: The Beacon Press.

Harcourt, G.C. 1972. *Some Cambridge Controversies in the Theory of Capital*. Cambridge: Cambridge University Press.

———. 1976. "The Cambridge Controversies: Old Ways and New Horizons—or Dead End?" *Oxford Economic Papers* 28, no. 1:25–65.

Hare, R.M. 1982. "Ethical Theory and Utilitarianism." In A. Sen and B. Williams, eds. *Utilitarianism and Beyond*.

Harper, J.W. 1910. *The Social Ideal and Dr. Chalmers' Contribution to Christian Economics*. Edinburgh: Macniven and Wallace.

Harrod, R.F. 1936. "Utilitarianism Revised." *Mind* 45:137–56.

———. [1938] 1950. "Scope and Method of Economics." *In Readings in Economic Analysis*. Ed. R.V. Clemence. Reading, MA: Addison-Wesley.

Harsanyi, J.C. 1982. "Morality and the Theory of Rational Behavior." In A. Sen and B. Williams, eds. *Utililitarianism and Beyond*.

Haslett, D.W. 1994. *Capitalism with Morality*. Oxford: Clarendon Press.

Hausman, D.M. 1984. *The Philosophy of Economics*. Cambridge: Cambridge University Press.

———. 1992. *The Inexact and Separate Science of Economics*. Cambridge: Cambridge University Press.

Hausman, D.M. and M.S. McPherson. 1993. "Taking Ethics Seriously: Economics and Contemporary Moral Philosophy." *Journal of Economic Literature* 31, no. 2:671–731.

Hayek, F.A. 1949. *Individualism and the Economic Order*. London: Routledge and Kegan Paul.

Heyne, P. 1978. "Economics and Ethics: The Problem of Dialogue." In W.W. Schroeder and G. Winter, eds. *Belief and Ethics*. Chicago: Center for the Scientific Study of Religion.

Hicks, J.R. 1939. "The Foundations of Welfare Economics." *Economic Journal* 49, no. 3:696–712.

———. [1939] 1946. *Value and Capital: An Inquiry into Some Fundamental Principles of Economic Theory*. Oxford: Clarendon Press.

_____. 1979. *Causality in Economics*. New York: Basic Books.

Hicks, J.R. and R.G.D. Allen. 1934. "A Reconsideration of the 'Theory of Value.' " *Economica* 1:52–76.

Hilton, B. 1988. *The Age of Atonement: The Influence of Evangelicalism on Social and Economic Thought, 1785–1865*. Oxford: Clarendon Press.

Hollis, M. and E. Nell. 1975. *Rational Economic Man: A Philosophical Critique of Neo-Classical Economics*. Cambridge: Cambridge University Press.

Hoover, K.D. 1988. *The New Classical Economics: A Skeptical Enquiry*. Oxford: Basil Blackwell.

Hume, D. [1752] 1817. *Essays Moral, Political and Literary*. Edinburgh. Reprinted in T.H. Green and T.H. Grose, eds. *The Philosophic Works*.

_____. 1964. *The Philosophic Works*. Ed. T.H. Green and T.H. Grose. Scientia Verlag Halen.

Hurley, S.L. 1989. *Natural Reasons: Personality and Policy*. Oxford: Oxford University Press.

Hutchison, T.W. [1938] 1960. *The Significance and Basic Postulates of Economic Theory*. New York: Kelley.

_____. 1953. *A Review of Economic Doctrines 1870–1929*. Oxford: Clarendon Press.

_____. 1964. *'Positive' Economics and Policy Objectives*. Cambridge, MA: Harvard University Press.

_____. 1977. *Knowledge and Ignorance in Economics*. Oxford: Basil Blackwell.

_____. 1978. *On revolutions and progress in economic knowledge*. Cambridge: Cambridge University Press.

_____. 1984. "Our Methodological Crisis." In P. Wiles et al., eds. *Economics in Disarray*. Oxford: Basil Blackwell.

_____. 1988. *Before Adam Smith: The Emergence of Political Economy, 1662–1776*. Oxford: Basil Blackwell.

_____. 1992. *Changing Aims in Economics*. Oxford: Basil Blackwell.

Huxley, A. [1938] 1965. *Ends and Means*. London: Chatto and Windus.

Hyma, A. 1951. *Renaissance to Reformation*. Grand Rapids: Eerdmans.

Jevons, W.S. [1871] 1957. *Theory of Political Economy*. New York: Kelley & Millman.

Johansen, L. 1976. "The Theory of Public Goods: Misplaced Emphasis." Oslo: Institute of Economics, University of Oslo.

Kaldor, N. 1939. "Welfare Propositions in Economics and Interpersonal Comparisons of Utility." *Economic Journal* 49, no. 3:549–52.

Kant, I. [1785] 1948. *The Moral Law*. Trans. H.J. Paton. London: Hutchinson.

_____. 1991. *Kant's Political Writings*. Ed. H. Reiss. Cambridge: Cambridge Unversity Press.

Katzner, D.W. 1986. "Potential Surprise, Potential Confirmation, and Probability." *Journal of Post Keynesian Economics* 9, no. 1:58–78.

_____. 1988. *Walrasian Microeconomics: An Introduction to the Economic Theory of Market Behavior*. Reading, MA: Addison-Wesley.

Keynes, J.M. [1931] 1972. *The Collected Writings of John Maynard Keynes*. London: Macmillan.

_____. 1936. *The General Theory of Employment, Interest and Money*. London: Macmillan.

_____ . [1937] 1947. "The General Theory of Employment." In S.E. Harris, ed. *The New Economics: Keynes' Influence on Theory and Public Policy.* London: Dennis Dobson.

_____ . 1956. *Essays and Sketches in Biography.* New York: Meridian Books.

Keynes, J.N. 1891. *The Scope and Method of Political Economy.* London: Macmillan.

Klappholz, K. [1964] 1984. "Value Judgments and Economics." *British Journal for the Philosophy of Science.* Reprinted in D.M. Hausman, ed. *The Philosophy of Economics.*

Kuhn, T. S. 1970. *The Structure of Scientific Revolutions.* Chicago: University of Chicago Press.

Lachmann, L.M. 1959. "Professor Shackle on the Economic Significance of Time." *Metroeconomica* 11:64–73.

Lakatos, I. 1970. "Falsification and the Methodology of Scientific Research Programmes." In I. Lakatos and A. Musgrave, eds. *Criticism and the Growth of Knowledge.*

Lakatos, I. and A. Musgrave, eds. 1970. *Criticism and the Growth of Knowledge.* Cambridge: Cambridge University Press.

Landreth, H. and D.C. Colander. 1989. *History of Economic Theory.* Boston: Houghton Mifflin.

Latsis, S.J., ed. 1976. *Method and Appraisal in Economics.* Cambridge: Cambridge University Press.

Leibenstein, H. 1960. *Economic Theory and Organizational Analysis.* New York: Harper & Row.

Lerner, A. 1946. *Economics of Control.* New York: Macmillan.

Letwin, W. 1963. *The Origins of Scientific Economics.* London: Methuen.

Little, I.M.D. 1950. *A Critique of Welfare Economics.* London: Oxford University Press.

Lloyd, W.F. 1834. *A Lecture on the Notion of Value, as Distinguishable not only from Utility but also from Value in Exchange.* London: Roake & Varty.

Locke, J. [1691] 1870. *Consequences of the lowering of interest, and raising the value of money and further considerations concerning raising the value of money* (1696). In J.R. McCulloch. *Principles of Political Economy.* London: Murray.

Luce, R.D. and H. Raiffa. 1957. *Games and Decisions: Introduction and Critical Survey.* New York: Wiley.

Mankiw, N.G. and D. Romer, eds. 1991. *New Keynesian Economics.* 2 vols. Cambridge, MA: MIT Press.

Marris, R. 1964. *The Economic Theory of Managerial Capitalism.* Glencoe, IL: Free Press.

Marshall, A. 1920. *Principles of Economics.* London: Macmillan.

McPherson, M.S. 1988. "Reuniting Economics and Philosophy." In G.C. Winston and R.F. Teichgraeber III, eds. *The Boundaries of Economics.* Cambridge: Cambridge University Press.

Melden, A.I., ed. 1967. *Ethical Theories: A Book of Readings.* Englewood Cliffs, NJ: Prentice-Hall.

Menger, C. [1871] 1950. *Grundsatze der Volkswirtschaftslehre.* Vienna: Braumuller. Trans. J. Dingwall and B.F. Hoselitz as *Principles of Economics.* Glencoe, IL: Free Press.

_____. [1883] 1985. *Studies in the Methods of the Social Sciences and of Political Economy in Particular*. Trans. F.J. Nock, Ed. L. White as *Investigations into the method of the social sciences with special reference to economics*. New York: New York University Press.

Midgley, M. 1993. "The Origin of Ethics." In P. Singer, ed. *A Companion to Ethics*. Oxford: Basil Blackwell.

Milgate, M. 1982. *Capital and Employment: A Study of Keynes's Economics*. London: Academic Press.

Mill, J.S. [1844] 1948. *Essays on Some Unsettled Questions of Political Economy*. London: London School of Economics and Political Science.

_____. [1848] 1961. *Principles of Political Economy*. Ed. W.J. Ashley. New York: Kelley.

_____. [1861] 1957. *Utilitarianism*. New York: Bobbs-Merrill.

Mirrlees, J.A. 1982. "The Economic Uses of Utilitarianism." In A. Sen and B. Williams, eds. *Utilitarianism and Beyond*.

Monsen, R.J. and A. Downs. 1965. "A Theory of Large Managerial Firms." *Journal of Political Economy* 73, no. 3:221–36.

Munby, D.L. 1963. *The Idea of a Secular Society and its Significance for Christians*. London: Oxford University Press.

Murray, J. 1957. *Principles of Conduct*. Grand Rapids: Eerdmans.

Myint, H.L.A. 1948. *Theories of Welfare Economics*. London: Longmans.

Myrdal, G. [1953] 1971. *The Political Element in the Development of Economic Theory*. London: Routledge & Kegan Paul.

_____. 1958. *Value in Social Theory: A Selection of Essays on Methodology*. Ed. P. Streeten. London: Routledge & Kegan Paul.

_____. 1961. "Value-loaded Concepts." In H. Hegeland, ed. *Money, Growth and Methodology: Essays in Honor of Johan Akerman*. Lund: Gleerup.

Niehans, J. 1990. *A History of Economic Theory: Classic Contributions, 1720–1980*. Baltimore: Johns Hopkins University Press.

Nozick, R. 1973. "Distributive Justice." *Philosophy and Public Affairs* 3.

_____. 1974. *Anarchy, State, and Utopia*. New York: Basic Books.

_____. 1993. *The Nature of Rationality*. Princeton: Princeton University Press.

O'Driscoll, G.P. and M.J. Rizzo. 1985. *The Economics of Time and Ignorance*. Oxford: Blackwell.

Osborne, D.K. 1964. "On the Goals of the Firm." *Quarterly Journal of Economics* 78, no. 4:592–603.

Pareto, V. [1909] 1971. *Manual of Political Economy*. Trans. A.S. Schwier. New York: Kelley.

Pigou, A.C. [1932] 1962. *The Economics of Welfare*. London: Macmillan.

_____. 1950. *The Veil of Money*. London: Macmillan.

Popper, K. 1959. *The Logic of Scientific Discovery*. New York: Basic Books.

Putterman, L. 1984. "On Some Recent Explanations of Why Capital Hires Labor." *Economic Inquiry* 22, no. 2:171–87.

_____. 1990. *Division of Labor and Welfare: An Introduction to Economic Systems*. Oxford: Oxford University Press.

Quesnay, F. [1759] 1972. *Tableau Économique*. Ed. R. Meek. Clifton, NJ: Kelley for the Royal Economic Society and the American Economic Association.

Raphael, D.D. 1975. "The Impartial Spectator." In A.S. Skinner and T. Wilson, eds. *Essays on Adam Smith.*

Rawls, J. 1971. *A Theory of Justice.* Cambridge, MA: Harvard University Press.

Regis, E. 1984. *Gewirth's Ethical Rationalism.* Chicago: University of Chicago Press.

Rescher, N. 1966. *Distributive Justice: A Constructive Critique of The Utilitarian Theory of Distribution.* Indianapolis: Bobbs-Merrill.

Resnick S. and R. Wolff, eds. 1985. *Rethinking Marxism: Struggles in Marxist Theory.* New York: Automedia.

_____. 1987. *Knowledge and Class: A Marxian Critique of Political Economy.* Chicago: University of Chicago Press.

Ricardo, D. [1817] 1911. *The Principles of Political Economy and Taxation.* M.P. Fogarty, ed. London: Dent and Sons.

_____. 1951–73. *The Works and Correspondence of David Ricardo.* 11 vols. P. Sraffa and M. Dobb, eds. Cambridge: Cambridge University Press.

Robbins, L. [1935] 1948. *An Essay on the Nature and Significance of Economic Science.* London: Macmillan.

_____. 1952. *The Theory of Economic Policy in English Classical Political Economy.* London: Macmillan.

Robertson, H.M. [1933] 1959. *Aspects of the Rise of Economic Individualism: A Criticism of Max Weber and his School.* New York: Kelley & Millman.

Robinson, J. [1933] 1969. *The Economics of Imperfect Competition.* London: Macmillan.

_____. 1962. *Economic Philosophy.* Chicago: Aldine Publishing Company.

Roemer, J.E. 1981. *Analytical Foundations of Marxian Economic Theory.* Cambridge: Cambridge University Press.

_____. 1982. *A General Theory of Exploitation and Class.* Cambridge, MA: Harvard University Press.

_____. 1985. *Value, Exploitation and Class.* London: Harvard Academic Publishers.

_____. 1988. *Free to Lose: An Introduction to Marxist Economic Philosophy.* Cambridge, MA: Harvard University Press.

_____. 1994. *Egalitarian Perspectives: Essays in Philosophic Economics.* Cambridge: Cambridge University Press.

_____, ed. 1986. *Analytical Marxism.* Cambridge: Cambridge University Press.

Rothschild, K.W. 1993. *Ethics and Economic Theory: Ideas, Models, Dilemmas.* London: Edward Elgar.

Samuels, W. 1988. "An Essay on the Nature and Significance of the Normative Nature of Economics." *Journal of Post Keynesian Economics* 10:3, 347–54.

Samuelson, P.A. 1937. "A Note on the Measurement of Utility." *Review of Economic Studies* 4:155–61.

_____. 1947. *Foundations of Economic Analysis.* Cambridge, MA: Harvard University Press.

_____. 1950. "Evaluation of Real National Income." *Oxford Economic Papers* 2, no. 1:1–29.

_____. 1958. "An Exact Consumption-Loan Model of Interest with or without the Social Contrivance of Money." *Journal of Political Economy* 66, no. 6:467–82.

Samuelsson, K. 1957. *Religion and Economic Action*. Trans. E.G. French. London: Heinemann.

Schneewind, J.B. 1977. *Sidgwick's Ethics and Victorian Moral Philosophy*. Oxford: Clarendon Press.

Schumpeter, J.A. [1934] 1961. *The Theory of Economic Development*. New York: Oxford University Press.

_____. 1954. *History of Economic Analysis*. New York: Oxford University Press.

Scitovsky, T. 1941. "A Note on Welfare Propositions in Economics." *Review of Economic Studies* 9:77–88.

Seligman, E.R.A. 1907. *The Economic Interpretation of History*. New York: Columbia University Press.

_____. 1925. *Essays in Economics*. New York: Macmillan.

Sen, A.K. [1970] 1979. "The Impossibility of a Paretian Liberal." *Journal of Political Economy* 78, no. 1:152–57. Reprinted in F. Hahn and M. Hollis, eds. *Philosophy and Economic Theory*.

_____. [1976–77] 1979. "Rational Fools: A Critique of the Behavioral Foundations of Economic Theory." *Philosophy and Public Affairs* 6:317–44. Reprinted in F. Hahn and M. Hollis, eds. *Philosophy and Economic Theory*.

_____. 1982. *Choice, Welfare and Measurement*. Cambridge, MA: MIT Press.

_____. 1987. *On Ethics and Economics*. Oxford: Basil Blackwell.

Sen, A.K. and B. Williams, eds. 1982. *Utilitarianism and Beyond*. Cambridge: Cambridge University Press.

Shackle, G.L.S. 1967. *The Years of High Theory: Invention and Tradition in Economic Thought 1926–1939*. Cambridge: Cambridge University Press.

_____. 1969. *Decision, Order, and Time in Human Affairs*. Cambridge: Cambridge University Press.

_____. 1972. *Epistemics and Economics: A Critique of Economic Doctrines*. Cambridge: Cambridge University Press.

Sidgwick, H. 1931. *Outlines of the History of Ethics*. London: Macmillan.

_____. [1874] 1962. *Methods of Ethics*. London: Macmillan.

_____. [1885] 1962. "The Scope and Method of Economic Science." In R.L. Smyth, ed. *Essays in Economic Method*. London: Duckworth.

Simon, H.A. 1972. "Theories of Bounded Rationality." In C.B. McGuire et al., eds. *Decision and Organization: A Volume in Honor of Jacob Marschak*. Amsterdam: North Holland.

Singer, P., ed. [1991] 1993. *A Companion to Ethics*. Oxford: Blackwell.

Skinner, A.S. 1975. Introduction to A.S. Skinner and T. Wilson, eds., *Essays on Adam Smith*.

Skinner, A.S. and T. Wilson, eds. *Essays on Adam Smith*. Oxford: Clarendon Press.

Smith, A. [1776] 1937. *An Inquiry into the Nature and Causes of the Wealth of Nations*. E. Cannan, ed. New York: Modern Library.

_____. 1976. *The Theory of Moral Sentiments*. In D.D. Raphael and A.L. Macfie, eds. *The Glasgow Edition of the Works and Correspondence of Adam Smith*, Vol. I. Oxford: Oxford University Press. Reprinted by Liberty Press, 1982.

Spiegel, H.W. 1991. *The Growth of Economic Thought*. Durham: Duke University Press.

Steuart, J. [1767] 1805. *An Inquiry into the Principles of Political Oeconomy.* 2 vols. London. Reprinted in *The Works: Political, Metaphysical and Chronological of Sir James Steuart.* 6 vols. London: Cadell and Davies.

Stigler, G. 1941. *Production and Distribution Theories.* New York: Macmillan.

Tawney, R.H. 1926. *Religion and the Rise of Capitalism.* New York: Harcourt Brace.

Tobin, J. 1958. "Liquidity Preference as Behavior Towards Risk." *Review of Economic Studies* 25:65–86.

———. 1972. "Inflation and Unemployment." *American Economic Review* 72, no. 1:1–18.

Van Til, C. 1974. *Christian Theistic Ethics.* Den Dulk Christian Foundation.

Varian, H.R. [1974–75] 1979. "Distributive Justice, Welfare Economics, and the Theory of Fairness." *Philosophy and Public Affairs* 4:223–47. Reprinted in F. Hahn and M. Hollis, eds. *Philosophy and Economic Theory.*

Vickers, D. 1959. *Studies in the Theory of Money 1690–1776.* Philadelphia: Chilton.

———. 1975. "Adam Smith and the Status of the Theory of Money." In A.S. Skinner and T. Wilson, eds. *Essays on Adam Smith.*

———. 1987. *Money Capital in the Theory of the Firm.* Cambridge: Cambridge University Press.

———. 1989. "The Illusion of the Economic Margin." *Journal of Post Keynesian Economics* 12, no. 1:88–97.

———. 1991. *The Long Run and the Short.* Bateman Memorial Lecture, University of Western Australia. Perth: Academic Press International.

———. 1994. *Economics and the Antagonism of Time: Time, Uncertainty, and Choice in Economic Theory.* Ann Arbor: University of Michigan Press.

———. 1995. *The Tyranny of the Market: A Critique of Theoretical Foundations.* Ann Arbor: University of Michigan Press.

Vickrey, W.S. 1945. "Measuring Marginal Utility by Reactions to Risk." *Econometrica* 13:319–33.

Viner, J. 1928. "Adam Smith and Laissez-faire." In *Adam Smith*, Ed. J.M. Clark. Chicago: University of Chicago Press.

———. 1972. *The Role of Providence in the Social Order.* Princeton: Princeton University Press.

———. 1978. *Religious Thought and Economic Society: Four Chapters of an Unfinished Work.* Ed. J. Melitz and D. Winch. Durham: Duke University Press.

von Neumann, J. and O. Morgenstern. [1944] 1947. *Theory of Games and Economic Behavior.* Princeton: Princeton University Press.

von Thünen, J.H. Part 1 1826. *Der Isolierte Staat.* Trans. C.M. Wartenberg, Ed. P. Hall. Oxford: Pergamon Press, 1966; Part 2, 1st section 1850. Trans. in B.W. Dempsey. *The Frontier Wage.* Chicago: Loyola University Press; Part 2, 2nd section 1863; Part 3. *Gründsatze zur Bestimmung der Bodenrente, der vorteilhaftesten Umtriebszeit und des Werts der Holzbestände von verschiedenem Alter fur Kieferqaldungen,* 1863.

Walras, L. [1874] 1969. *Elements of Pure Economics.* New York: Kelley.

Walsh, V. 1987. "Philosophy and Economics." In J. Eatwell, M. Milgate, and P. Newman, eds. *The New Palgrave: A Dictionary of Economics.*

Waterman, A.M.C. 1991. *Revolution, Economics and Religion: Christian Political Economy, 1798–1833.* Cambridge: Cambridge University Press.

Weber, M. [1904–5] 1958. *The Protestant Ethic and the Spirit of Capitalism.* Trans. T. Parsons. New York: Charles Scribner's Sons.

———. 1949. *The Methodology of the Social Sciences.* Trans. and ed. E.A. Shilz and H.A. Finch. Glencoe, IL: Free Press. Excerpted in D.M. Hausman, ed. *The Philosophy of Economics: An Anthology.*

———. 1984. "Objectivity and Understanding in Economics." In D.M. Hausman, ed. *The Philosophy of Economics: An Anthology.*

Weisskopf, W.A. 1977. "The Moral Predicament of the Market Economy." In G. Dworkin, G. Bermant, and P.G. Brown, eds. *Markets and Morals.* Washington: Hemisphere Publishing Corporation.

Weitzman, M.L. 1983. "Some Macroeconomic Implications of Alternative Compensation Systems." *Economic Journal* 93:763–83.

———. 1984. *The Share Economy.* Cambridge, MA: Harvard University Press.

Welch, C. 1987. "Utilitarianism." In J. Eatwell, M. Milgate, and P. Newman, eds. *The New Palgrave: A Dictionary of Economics.*

Weston, S.C. 1994. "Toward a Better Understanding of the Positive/Normative Distinction in Economics." *Economics and Philosophy* 10,1: no. 1–17.

Wicksteed, P.H. [1894] 1932. *Essay on the Coordination of the Laws of Distribution.* London: London School of Economics and Political Science.

———. [1910] 1950. *The Common Sense of Political Economy and Selected Papers and Reviews on Economic Theory.* 2 vols. Ed. L. Robbins. London: Routledge and Kegan Paul.

Williamson, O.E. 1964. *The Economics of Discretionary Behavior: Managerial Objectives in a Theory of the Firm.* Englewood Cliffs, NJ: Prentice-Hall.

Wolff, R.P. 1977. *Understanding Rawls: A Reconstruction and Critique of "A Theory of Justice."* Princeton: Princeton University Press.

INDEX

ABOUT THE AUTHOR

DOUGLAS VICKERS, Professor Emeritus of Economics, University of Massachusetts, Amherst, has held positions with universities in the United States and Australia and has served with the National Bank of Australasia and Vauxhall Motors Ltd. Among his fourteen earlier books are *The Tyranny of the Market* and *Money Capital in the Theory of the Firm*.

ISBN 0-275-95978-3

9 0 0 0 0 >

EAN

9 780275 959784

HARDCOVER BAR CODE